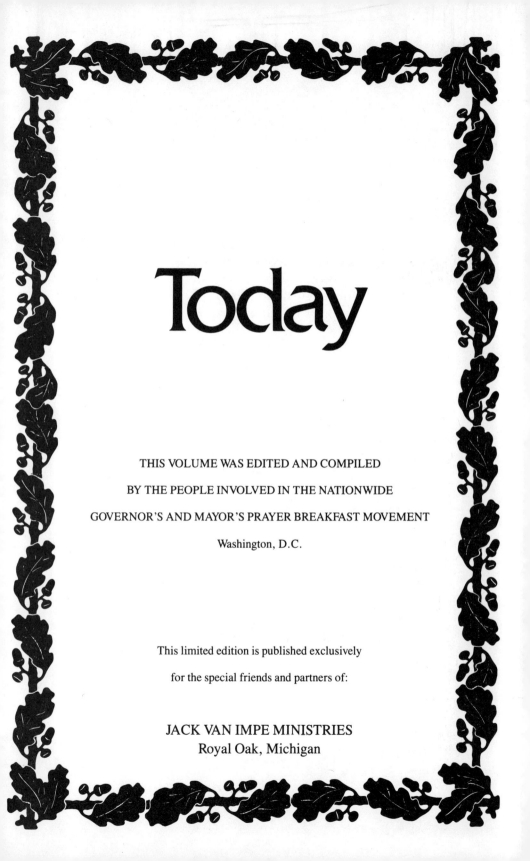

Today

THIS VOLUME WAS EDITED AND COMPILED

BY THE PEOPLE INVOLVED IN THE NATIONWIDE

GOVERNOR'S AND MAYOR'S PRAYER BREAKFAST MOVEMENT

Washington, D.C.

This limited edition is published exclusively

for the special friends and partners of:

JACK VAN IMPE MINISTRIES
Royal Oak, Michigan

We have not been able to include all
Scripture passages in their entirety.
We would encourage you to refer to
your own Bible to read the entire
chapters which are quoted from here.

Published in Nashville, Tennessee, by Thomas Nelson, Inc. and distrib-
uted in Canada by Lawson Falle, Ltd., Cambridge, Ontario.

Printed in the United States of America.

Second printing

All Scripture verses are from the King James Version of the Bible.

Library of Congress Cataloging in Publication Data

Main entry under title:

Today.

  Bibliography: p.
  1. Christian life—Quotations, maxims, etc.
BV4513.T6   242   77-27661
ISBN 0-8407-5130-3

Dedicated to those in positions of great responsibility who so often experience an overpowering loneliness, accompanied by a lack of understanding, in the midst of the multitude.

Foreword

I love the Word of God. There is no other literature the Lord has for nurturing His saints. Everything Christians are or ever hope to be comes as a result of studying the blessed Book the Holy Spirit wrote (II Peter 1:21).

The Word produces victory over sin (Psalm 119:11), it makes believers clean (John 15:3), it produces and increases faith (Romans 10:17), and it brings blessings (Revelation 1:3).

Recently Rexella and I went through a book entitled *Today*, for devotions. The blessings we derived from this scripturally-packed volume were inestimable. Never have we been as stirred and moved as we were by this subject-oriented arrangement of Scripture. Because of it, Rexella and I chose this special Christmas gift for you. May you be as blessed as we were.

We love you.

Jack Van Impe

God

Posterity will some day laugh at the foolishness of modern materialistic philosophy. The more I study nature, the more I am amazed at the Creator.

—*Louis Pasteur*

I give myself over to rapture. I tremble; my blood leaps. God has waited six thousand years for a looker–on to His work. His wisdom is infinite; that of which we are ignorant is contained in Him, as well as the little that we know.

—*Johann Kepler*

It is impossible to account for the creation of the universe, without the agency of a Supreme Being.

—*George Washington*

Here is my creed. I believe in one God, Creator of the Universe. That He governs it by His providence. That He ought to be worshiped. That the most acceptable service we render Him is doing good to His other children.

—*Benjamin Franklin*

There is a God. The plants of the valley, the cedars of the mountain bless His name; the elephant salutes Him with the rising day; the bird glorifies Him among the foliage; the lightning bespeaks His power, and the ocean declares His immensity. Man alone has said, "There is no God."

—*Vicomte de Chauteaubriand*

The wise of all the earth have said in their hearts always, "God is, and there is none beside Him"; and the fools of all the earth have said in their hearts always, "I am, and there is none beside me."

—*John Ruskin*

Genesis

1 In the beginning God created the heaven and the earth.

2 And the earth was without form, and void; and the darkness *was* upon the face of the deep. And the Spirit of God moved upon the face of the waters.

3 And God said, Let there be light: and there was light.

4 And God saw the light, that *it was* good: and God divided the light from the darkness.

5 And God called the light Day, and the darkness he called Night. And the evening and the morning were the first day.

6 And God said, Let there be a firmament in the midst of the waters, and let it divide the waters from the waters.

8 And God called the firmament Heaven. And the evening and the morning were the second day.

9 And God said, Let the waters under the heaven be gathered together unto one place, and let the dry *land* appear: and it was so.

10 And God called the dry *land* Earth; and the gathering together of the waters called he Seas: and God saw that *it was* good.

11 And God said, Let the earth bring forth grass, the herb yielding seed, *and* the fruit tree yielding fruit after his kind, whose seed *is* in itself, upon the earth: and it was so.

13 And the evening and the morning were the third day.

14 And God said, Let there be lights in the firmament of the heaven to divide the day from the night; and let them be for signs, and for seasons, and for days, and years:

15 And let them be for lights in the firmament of the heaven to give light upon the earth: and it was so.

16 And God made two great lights; the greater light to rule the day, and the lesser light to rule the night: *he made* the stars also.

19 And the evening and the morning were the fourth day.

20 And God said, Let the waters bring forth abundantly the moving creature that hath life, and fowl *that* may fly above the earth in the open firmament of heaven.

21 And God created great whales, and every living creature that moveth, which the waters brought forth abundantly, after their kind, and every winged fowl after his kind: and God saw that *it was* good.

23 And the evening and the morning were the fifth day.

24 And God said, Let the earth bring forth the living creature after his kind, cattle, and creeping thing, and beast of the earth after his kind: and it was so.

25 And God made the beast of the earth after his kind, and cattle after their kind, and every thing that creepeth upon the earth after his kind: and God saw that *it was* good.

God created everything and it was all good.

If the Father deigns to touch with divine power the cold and pulseless heart of the buried acorn and to make it burst forth from its prison walls, will He leave neglected in the earth the soul of man made in the image of his Creator?

—*William Jennings Bryan*

I could prove God statistically. Take the human body alone—the chance that all the functions of the individual would just happen is a statistical monstrosity.

—*George Gallup*

No sin is small. It is against an infinite God, and may have consequences immeasurable.

—*Jeremy Taylor*

Man seeks his own good at the whole world's cost.

—*Robert Browning*

Corruption is natural in government because it is natural in man.

—*Will Durant*

The hour has struck for our "conversion," for personal transformation, for interior renewal. We must get used to thinking of man in a new way; and in a new way also of man's life in common; with a new manner, too, of conceiving the paths of history and the destiny of the world, according to the words of St. Paul: "You must be clothed in the new self, which is created in God's image, justified and sanctified through the truth."

—*Pope Paul VI*

Genesis

8 And the Lord God planted a garden eastward in Eden; and there he put the man whom he had formed.

9 And out of the ground made the Lord God to grow every tree that is pleasant to the sight, and good for food; the tree of life also in the midst of the garden, and the tree of knowledge of good and evil.

16 And the Lord God commanded the man, saying, Of every tree of the garden thou mayest freely eat:

17 But of the tree of the knowledge of good and evil, thou shalt not eat of it: for in the day that thou eatest thereof thou shalt surely die.

18 And the Lord God said, *It is* not good that the man should be alone; I will make him an help meet for him.

21 And the Lord God caused a deep sleep to fall upon Adam, and he slept: and he took one of his ribs, and closed up the flesh instead thereof;

22 And the rib, which the Lord God had taken from man, made he a woman, and brought her unto the man.

23 And Adam said, This *is* now bone of my bones, and flesh of my flesh: she shall be called Woman, because she was taken out of Man.

24 Therefore shall a man leave his father and his mother, and shall cleave unto his wife: and they shall be one flesh.

CHAPTER 3

1 Now the serpent was more subtil than any beast of the field which the Lord God had made. And he said unto the woman, Yea, hath God said, Ye shall not eat of every tree of the garden?

2 And the woman said unto the serpent, We may eat of the fruit of the trees of the garden:

3 But of the fruit of the tree which *is* in the midst of the garden, God hath said, Ye shall not eat of it, neither shall ye touch it, lest ye die.

4 And the serpent said unto the woman, Ye shall not surely die:

5 For God doth know that in the day ye eat thereof, then your eyes shall be opened, and ye shall be as gods, knowing good and evil.

6 And when the woman saw that the tree *was* good for food, and that it *was* pleasant to the eyes, and a tree to be desired to make *one* wise, she took of the fruit thereof, and did eat, and gave also unto her husband with her; and he did eat.

7 And the eyes of them both were opened, and they knew that they *were* naked; and they sewed fig leaves together, and made themselves aprons.

8 And they heard the voice of the Lord God walking in the garden in the cool of the day: and Adam and his wife hid themselves from the presence of the Lord God amongst the trees of the garden.

Sin will ruin the most perfect situation.

Without commandments, obliging us to live after a certain fashion, our existence is that of the "unemployed." This is the terrible situation in which the best youth of the world finds itself today. By dint of feeling itself free, exempt from restrictions, it feels itself empty.

—*José Ortega y Gasset*

Spiritual truth is more essential to a nation than mortar to its cities' walls. For when the actions of a people are unguided by these truths, it is only a matter of time before the walls themselves collapse.

—*Charles Lindbergh*

Some time ago Steinmetz, the wizard of power resources, wrote to Babson, the wizard of business movements: "The greatest power of all is in our midst unscratched today. I refer to the spiritual power that comes through right living and worship. Our fathers knew the power of prayer, the economic importance of Sabbath observance, and the need of family and public worship. To this fact America owes its growth. Today this power is temporarily forgotten. Some day it will be harnessed. Then America will be truly healthy, happy, and safe."

—*Unknown*

Study history and learn one thing: he who thinks he can cheat a moral God in a moral universe is a moral imbecile. It simply cannot be done. Evil carries the seeds of its own destruction within it. The universe is not built for the success of lies. They break themselves upon the moral facts of the universe. The Lord reigneth—whether that reign is acknowledged or not. Every wrong breaks itself upon the fact of God.

—*E. Stanley Jones*

I find the great thing in this world is not so much where we stand, as in what direction we are moving.

—*Oliver Wendell Holmes, Sr.*

Exodus

1 And God spake all these words, saying,

2 I *am* the Lord thy God, which have brought thee out of the land of Egypt, out of the house of bondage.

3 Thou shalt have no other gods before me.

4 Thou shalt not make unto thee any graven image, or any likeness *of any thing* that *is* in heaven above, or that *is* in the earth beneath, or that *is* in the water under the earth:

5 Thou shalt not bow down thyself to them, nor serve them: for I the Lord thy God *am* a jealous God, visiting the iniquity of the fathers upon the children unto the third and fourth *generation* of them that hate me;

6 And showing mercy unto thousands of them that love me, and keep my commandments.

7 Thou shalt not take the name of the Lord thy God in vain: for the Lord will not hold him guiltless that taketh his name in vain.

8 Remember the sabbath day, to keep it holy.

9 Six days shalt thou labor, and do all thy work:

10 But the seventh day *is* the sabbath of the Lord thy God: *in it* thou shalt not do any work, thou, nor thy son, nor thy daughter, thy manservant, nor thy maidservant, nor thy cattle, nor thy stranger that *is* within thy gates:

11 For *in* six days the Lord made heaven and earth, the sea, and all that in them *is,* and rested the seventh day: wherefore the Lord blessed the sabbath day, and hallowed it.

12 Honor thy father and thy mother: that thy days may be long upon the land which the Lord thy God giveth thee.

13 Thou shalt not kill.

14 Thou shalt not commit adultery.

15 Thou shalt not steal.

16 Thou shalt not bear false witness against thy neighbor.

17 Thou shalt not covet thy neighbor's house, thou shalt not covet thy neighbor's wife, nor his manservant, nor his maidservant, nor his ox, nor his ass, nor any thing that *is* thy neighbor's.

18 And all the people saw the thunderings, and the lightnings, and the noise of the trumpet, and the mountain smoking: and when the people saw *it* they removed, and stood afar off.

19 And they said unto Moses, Speak thou with us, and we will hear: but let not God speak with us, lest we die.

20 And Moses said unto the people, Fear not: for God is come to prove you, and that his fear may be before your faces, that ye sin not.

Obey God—and live.

There is nothing which God cannot accomplish.

—*Cicero*

We mortals are on board a fast-sailing, never-sinking world-frigate, of which God was the ship-wright; and she is but one craft in a Milky-Way fleet, of which God is the Lord High Admiral. The port we sail from is always astern.

—*Herman Melville*

Nasr-ed-Din Hodja, in the heat of the day, sat under a walnut tree looking at his pumpkin vines. He said to himself, "How foolish God is! Here He puts a great heavy pumpkin on a tiny vine without strength to do anything but lie on the ground. And He puts a tiny walnut on a tree whose branches could hold the weight of a man. If I were God, I could do a better job than that!" Just then a breeze dislocated a walnut in the tree, and it fell on the head of skeptical Nasr-ed-Din Hodja, who rubbed his head, a sadder and a wiser man. "Suppose," he mused, "there had been a pumpkin up there, instead of a walnut. Never again will I try to plan the world for God, but I shall thank God that He has done so well."

—*Frank C. Mead*

God is not a cosmic bell-boy for whom we can press a button to get things done.

—*Harry Emerson Fosdick*

Thou art my Master and my Author; Thou alone art He from whom I took the good style that hath done me honor.

—*Dante*

He is the greatest Artist who has embodied, in the sum of His works, the greatest number of the greatest ideas.

—*John Ruskin*

Job

1 Then the LORD answered Job out of the whirlwind, and said,

2 Who *is* this that darkeneth counsel by words without knowledge?

3 Gird up now thy loins like a man; for I will demand of thee, and answer thou me.

4 Where wast thou when I laid the foundations of the earth? declare, if thou hast understanding.

5 Who hath laid the measures thereof, if thou knowest? or who hath stretched the line upon it?

6 Whereupon are the foundations thereof fastened? or who laid the corner stone thereof;

7 When the morning stars sang together, and all the sons of God shouted for joy?

8 Or *who* shut up the sea with doors, when it brake forth, *as if* it had issued out of the womb?

9 When I made the cloud the garment thereof, and thick darkness a swaddling band for it,

10 And brake up for it my decreed *place,* and set bars and doors,

11 And said, Hitherto shalt thou come, but no further: and here shall thy proud waves be stayed?

17 Have the gates of death been opened unto thee? or hast thou seen the doors of the shadow of death?

18 Hast thou perceived the breadth of the earth? declare if thou knowest it all.

19 Where *is* the way *where* light dwelleth? and *as for* darkness, where *is* the place thereof,

20 That thou shouldest take it to the bound thereof, and that thou shouldest know the paths *to* the house thereof?

21 Knowest thou *it,* because thou wast then born? or *because* the number of thy days *is* great?

22 Hast thou entered into the treasures of the snow? or hast thou seen the treasures of the hail,

23 Which I have reserved against the time of trouble, against the day of battle and war?

28 Hath the rain a father? or who hath begotten the drops of dew?

29 Out of whose womb came the ice? and the hoary frost of heaven, who hath gendered it?

CHAPTER 42

1 Then Job answered the LORD, and said,

2 I know that thou canst do every *thing,* and *that* no thought can be withholden from thee.

3 Who *is* he that hideth counsel without knowledge? therefore have I uttered that I understood not; things too wonderful for me, which I knew not.

4 Hear, I beseech thee, and I will speak: I will demand of thee, and declare thou unto me.

5 I have heard of thee by the hearing of the ear; but now mine eye seeth thee:

6 Wherefore I abhor *myself,* and repent in dust and ashes.

The greatness of God is beyond our comprehension.

When I think of God, my heart is so full of joy that the notes leap and dance as they leave my pen; and since God has given me a cheerful heart, I serve Him with a cheerful spirit.

—*Franz Joseph Haydn*

A man should be encouraged to do what the Maker of him has intended by the making of him, according as the gifts have been bestowed on him for that purpose. His happiness, and that of others around him [depends upon] such a relation to the Maker's will.

—*Thomas Carlyle*

If we who serve free men today are to differ from the tyrants of this age, we must balance the powers in our hands with God in our hearts.

—*Lyndon B. Johnson*

Man is really three persons in one: what people think he is, what he sees himself to be, and what God really knows him to be.

—*W. L. Childress*

When we return to real trust in God, there will no longer be room in our souls for fear.

—*Goethe*

When you have shut your doors, and darkened your room, remember never to say that you are alone; for God is within and your genius is within, and what need have they of light to see what you are doing?

—*Epictetus*

Psalms

1 O Lord, thou hast searched me, and known *me*.

2 Thou knowest my downsitting and mine uprising; thou understandest my thought afar off.

3 Thou compassest my path and my lying down, and art acquainted *with* all my ways.

4 For *there is* not a word in my tongue, *but,* lo, O Lord, thou knowest it altogether.

5 Thou hast beset me behind and before, and laid thine hand upon me.

6 *Such* knowledge *is* too wonderful for me; it is high, I cannot *attain* unto it.

7 Whither shall I go from thy Spirit? or whither shall I flee from thy presence?

8 If I ascend up into heaven, thou *art* there: if I make my bed in hell, behold, thou *art there.*

9 *If* I take the wings of the morning, *and* dwell in the uttermost parts of the sea;

10 Even there shall thy hand lead me, and thy right hand shall hold me.

11 If I say, Surely the darkness shall cover me; even the night shall be light about me.

12 Yea, the darkness hideth not from thee; but the night shineth as the day: the darkness and the light *are* both alike *to thee.*

13 For thou hast possessed my reins: thou hast covered me in my mother's womb.

14 I will praise thee; for I am fearfully *and* wonderfully made: marvelous *are* thy works; and *that* my soul knoweth right well.

15 My substance was not hid from thee when I was made in secret, *and* curiously wrought in the lowest parts of the earth.

16 Thine eyes did see my substance, yet being unperfect; and in thy book all *my members* were written, *which* in continuance were fashioned, when *as yet there was* none of them.

17 How precious also are thy thoughts unto me, O God! how great is the sum of them!

18 *If* I should count them, they are more in number than the sand: when I awake, I am still with thee.

19 Surely thou wilt slay the wicked, O God: depart from me therefore, ye bloody men.

20 For they speak against thee wickedly, *and* thine enemies take *thy name* in vain.

21 Do not I hate them, O Lord, that hate thee? and am not I grieved with those that rise up against thee?

22 I hate them with perfect hatred: I count them mine enemies.

23 Search me, O God, and know my heart: try me, and know my thoughts:

24 And see if *there be any* wicked way in me, and lead me in the way everlasting.

God knows you intimately.

When the fulness of time was come, God sent forth His Son.

—*Galatians 4:4*

God's plans, like lilies
    Pure and white unfold:
We must not tear the close
    shut leaves apart;
Time will reveal the calyxes of gold.

—*May Riley Smith*

And God said, Let there be light: and there was light.

—*Genesis 1:3*

God answers prayer in the best way, not sometimes, but every time, although the immediate manifestation of the answer in the domain in which we want it may not always follow.

—*Oswald Chambers*

The secret of success in life is for a man to be ready for his opportunity when it comes.

—*Benjamin Disraeli*

Is anything too hard for the Lord? At the time appointed I will return unto thee. . . .

—*Genesis 18:14*

He who hath heard the Word of God can bear His silences.

—*Ignatius of Loyola*

Think of the enormous leisure of God! He is never in a hurry.

—*Oswald Chambers*

Ecclesiastes

1 To every *thing there is* a season, and a time to every purpose under the heaven:

2 A time to be born, and a time to die; a time to plant, and a time to pluck up *that which is* planted:

3 A time to kill, and a time to heal; a time to break down, and a time to build up;

4 A time to weep, and a time to laugh; a time to mourn, and a time to dance;

5 A time to cast away stones, and a time to gather stones together; a time to embrace, and a time to refrain from embracing;

6 A time to get, and a time to lose; a time to keep, and a time to cast away;

7 A time to rend, and a time to sew; a time to keep silence, and a time to speak;

8 A time to love, and a time to hate; a time of war, and a time of peace.

9 What profit hath he that worketh in that wherein he laboreth?

10 I have seen the travail, which God hath given to the sons of men to be exercised in it.

11 He hath made every *thing* beautiful in his time: also he hath set the world in their heart, so that no man can find out the work that God maketh from the beginning to the end.

14 I know that, whatsoever God doeth, it shall be for ever: nothing can be put to it, nor any thing taken from it: and God doeth *it,* that *men* should fear before him.

15 That which hath been is now; and that which is to be hath already been; and God requireth that which is past.

16 And moreover I saw under the sun the place of judgment, *that* wickedness *was* there; and the place of righteousness, *that* iniquity *was* there.

17 I said in mine heart, God shall judge the righteous and the wicked: for *there is* a time there for every purpose and for every work.

18 I said in mine heart concerning the estate of the sons of men, that God might manifest them, and that they might see that they themselves are beasts.

19 For that which befalleth the sons of men befalleth beasts; even one thing befalleth them: as the one dieth, so dieth the other; yea, they have all one breath; so that a man hath no preeminence above a beast: for all *is* vanity.

20 All go unto one place; all are of the dust, and all turn to dust again.

21 Who knoweth the spirit of man that goeth upward, and the spirit of the beast that goeth downward to the earth?

22 Wherefore I perceive that *there* is nothing better, than that a man should rejoice in his own works; for that *is* his portion: for who shall bring him to see what shall be after him?

God's timing, not ours, is what is important.

The things that are wrong with the country today are the sum total of all the things that are wrong with us as individuals.

—*Charles W. Tobey*

Man proposes, but God disposes.

—*Thomas à Kempis*

We have been the recipients of the choicest bounties of heaven; we have been preserved these many years in peace and prosperity; we have grown in number, wealth, and power as no other nation has ever grown. But we have forgotten God! Intoxicated with unbroken success, we have become too self-sufficient to feel the necessity of redeeming and preserving grace, too proud to pray to the God who made us.

—*Abraham Lincoln*

We live, my dear sir, in times that furnish abundant matter for serious and profound reflections. It is a consolatory one that every scourge of every kind by which nations are punished or corrected is under the control of a wise and benevolent Sovereign.

—*John Jay*

My great concern is not whether God is on our side; my great concern is to be on God's side.

—*Abraham Lincoln*

Be not angry that you cannot make others as you wish them to be, since you cannot make yourself as you wish to be.

—*Thomas à Kempis*

I have lived, Sir, a long time, and the longer I live, the more convincing proofs I see of this truth—that God governs in the affairs of men. And if a sparrow cannot fall to the ground without His notice, is it probable that an empire can arise without His aid?

—*Benjamin Franklin*

Isaiah

5 I *am* the LORD, and *there* is none else, *there is* no God besides me: I girded thee, though thou hast not known me;

6 That they may know from the rising of the sun, and from the west, that *there is* none besides me. I *am* the LORD, and *there is* none else.

9 Woe unto him that striveth with his Maker! *Let* the potsherd *strive* with the potsherds of the earth. Shall the clay say to him that fashioneth it, What makest thou? or thy work, He hath no hands?

10 Woe unto him that saith unto *his* father, What begettest thou? or to the woman, What hast thou brought forth?

11 Thus saith the LORD, the Holy One Of Israel, and his Maker, Ask me of things to come concerning my sons, and concerning the work of my hands command ye me.

12 I have made the earth, and created man upon it: I, *even* my hands, have stretched out the heavens, and all their host have I commanded.

13 I have raised him up in righteousness, and I will direct all his ways: he shall build my city, and he shall let go my captives, not for price nor reward, saith the LORD of hosts.

15 Verily thou *art* a God that hidest thyself, O God of Israel, the Saviour.

16 They shall be ashamed, and also confounded, all of them: they shall go to confusion together *that are* makers of idols.

17 *But* Israel shall be saved in the LORD with an everlasting salvation: ye shall not be ashamed nor confounded world without end.

18 For thus saith the LORD that created the heavens; God himself that formed the earth and made it; he hath established it, he created it not in vain, he formed it to be inhabited: I *am* the LORD, and *there* is none else.

19 I have not spoken in secret, in a dark place of the earth: I said not unto the seed of Jacob, Seek ye me in vain: I the LORD speak righteousness, I declare things that are right.

20 Assemble yourselves and come; draw near together, ye *that are* escaped of the nations: they have no knowledge that set up the wood of their graven image, and pray unto a god *that* cannot save.

22 Look unto me, and be ye saved, all the ends of the earth: for I *am* God, and *there is* none else.

23 I have sworn by myself, the word is gone out of my mouth *in* righteousness, and shall not return, That unto me every knee shall bow, every tongue shall swear.

24 Surely shall *one* say, In the LORD have I righteousness and strength: *even* to him shall *men* come; and all that are incensed against him shall be ashamed.

25 In the LORD shall all the seed of Israel be justified, and shall glory.

God is in the business of building men and nations.

The best proof of God's existence is what follows when we deny it.

—*William L. Sullivan*

For every civilization or every period of history it is true today: Show me what kind of God you have and I will tell you what kind of humanity you possess.

—*Emil Brunner*

Sometimes a nation abolishes God, but fortunately God is more tolerant.

—*Unknown*

Without some moral and spiritual awakening, we will awaken some morning to find ourselves disappearing in the dust of an atomic explosion.

—*Dwight Eisenhower*

The sum of the whole matter is this: If our civilization is to survive materially, it must be redeemed spiritually.

—*Woodrow Wilson*

Men will either be governed by God or ruled by tyrants.

—*William Penn*

Men are qualified for civil liberties in exact proportion to their disposition to put moral chains on their own appetites. . . . Society cannot exist unless a controlling power upon will and appetite is placed somewhere, and the less of it there is within, the more there must be without. It is ordained in the eternal constitution of things that men of intemperate minds cannot be free. Their passions forge their fetters.

—*Edmund Burke*

Romans

18 For the wrath of God is revealed from heaven against all ungodliness and unrighteousness of men, who hold the truth in unrighteousness;

20 For the invisible things of him from the creation of the world are clearly seen, being understood by the things that are made, *even* his eternal power and Godhead; so that they are without excuse:

21 Because that, when they knew God, they glorified *him* not as God, neither were thankful; but became vain in their imaginations, and their foolish heart was darkened.

22 Professing themselves to be wise, they became fools,

24 Wherefore God also gave them up to uncleanness, through the lusts of their own hearts, to dishonor their own bodies between themselves:

25 Who changed the truth of God into a lie, and worshipped and served the creature more than the Creator, who is blessed for ever. Amen.

28 And even as they did not like to retain God in *their* knowledge, God gave them over to a reprobate mind, to do those things which are not convenient;

29 Being filled with all unrighteousness, fornication, wickedness, covetousness, maliciousness; full of envy, murder, debate, deceit, malignity; whisperers,

30 Backbiters, haters of God, despiteful, proud, boasters, inventors of evil things, disobedient to parents,

31 Without understanding, covenantbreakers, without natural affection, implacable, unmerciful:

32 Who, knowing the judgment of God, that they which commit such things are worthy of death, not only do the same, but have pleasure in them that do them.

CHAPTER 2

1 Therefore thou art inexcusable, O man, whosoever thou art that judgest: for wherein thou judgest another, thou condemnest thyself; for thou that judgest doest the same things.

2 But we are sure that the judgment of God is according to truth against them which commit such things.

3 And thinkest thou this, O man, that judgest them which do such things, and doest the same, that thou shalt escape the judgment of God?

4 Or despisest thou the riches of his goodness and forbearance and longsuffering; not knowing that the goodness of God leadeth thee to repentance?

5 But, after thy hardness and impenitent heart, treasurest up unto thyself wrath against the day of wrath and revelation of the righteous judgment of God;

6 Who will render to every man according to his deeds.

Rebellion against God means the ruin of a people.

All the strength and force of a man comes from his faith in things unseen.

—*James Freeman Clarke*

More persons, on the whole, are humbugged by believing in nothing, than by believing too much.

—*Phineas T. Barnum*

Faith is the daring of the soul to go farther than it can see.

—*William Newton Clarke*

All work that is worth anything is done in faith.

—*Albert Schweitzer*

Whoso draws nigh to God one step through doubtings dim, God will advance a mile in blazing light to him.

—*Unknown*

The man who listens to reason is lost: Reason enslaves all whose minds are not strong enough to master her.

—*George Bernard Shaw*

God does not die on the day when we cease to believe in a personal diety, but we die on the day when our lives cease to be illumined by the steady radiance, renewed daily, of a Wonder, the Source of which is beyond all reason.

—*Dag Hammarskjold*

The promises of God are just as good as ready money any day.

—*Billy Bray*

Hebrews

1 Now faith is the substance of things hoped for, the evidence of things not seen.

3 Through faith we understand that the worlds were framed by the word of God, so that things which are seen were not made of things which do appear.

6 But without faith *it is* impossible to please *him:* for he that cometh to God must believe that he is, and *that* he is a rewarder of them that diligently seek him.

7 By faith Noah, being warned of God of things not seen as yet, moved with fear, prepared an ark to the saving of his house; by the which he condemned the world, and became heir of the righteousness which is by faith.

8 By faith Abraham, when he was called to go out into a place which he should after receive for an inheritance, obeyed; and he went out, not knowing whither he went.

9 By faith he sojourned in the land of promise, as *in* a strange country, dwelling in tabernacles with Isaac and Jacob, the heirs with him of the same promise:

10 For he looked for a city which hath foundations, whose builder and maker *is* God.

11 Through faith also Sarah herself received strength to conceive seed, and was delivered of a child when she was past age, because she judged him faithful who had promised.

13 These all died in faith, not having received the promises, but having seen them afar off, and were persuaded of *them,* and embraced *them* and confessed that they were strangers and pilgrims on the earth.

32 And what shall I more say? for the time would fail me to tell of Gideon, and *of* Barak, and *of* Samson, and *of* Jephthah; *of* David also, and Samuel, and *of* the prophets:

33 Who through faith subdued kingdoms, wrought righteousness, obtained promises, stopped the mouths of lions,

34 Quenched the violence of fire, escaped the edge of the sword, out of weakness were made strong, waxed valiant in fight, turned to flight the armies of the aliens.

35 Women received their dead raised to life again: and others were tortured, not accepting deliverance; that they might obtain a better resurrection:

36 And others had trial of *cruel* mockings and scourgings, yea, moreover of bonds and imprisonment:

38 Of whom the world was not worthy: they wandered in deserts, and *in* mountains, and *in* dens and caves of the earth.

39 And these all, having obtained a good report through faith, received not the promise:

40 God having provided some better thing for us, that they without us should not be made perfect.

The object of true faith is God.

Reflections

The Highest
Purpose of Man

If we work upon marble, it will perish. If we work upon brass, time will efface it. If we rear temples, they will crumble to dust. But, if we work upon men's immortal minds, if we imbue them with high principles, with the just fear of God, with love of their fellow men, we engrave on those tablets something which no time can efface and which will brighten and brighten to all eternity.

—Daniel Webster

The study of God's Word, for the purpose of discovering God's will, is the secret discipline which has formed the greatest characters.

—J. W. Alexander

Being a humble instrument in the hands of our heavenly Father, I desire that all my words and acts may be according to His will; and that it may be so, I give thanks to the Almighty, and seek His aid.

—Abraham Lincoln

Nurture your mind with great thoughts.

—Benjamin Disraeli

If you see a man unterrified in the midst of dangers, untouched by desires, happy in adversity, peaceful amid the storm, will you not say: a divine power has descended upon that man?

—Seneca

When any church will inscribe over its altars, as its sole qualification for membership, the Savior's condensed statement for the substance of both law and gospel. "Thou shalt love the Lord thy God with all thy heart, and with all thy soul, and with all thy mind," and ". . . thy neighbor as thyself," that church will I join with all my heart and soul.

—Abraham Lincoln

Deuteronomy

1 Now these *are* the commandments, the statutes, and the judgments, which the LORD your God commanded to teach you, that ye might do *them* in the land whither ye go to possess it:

2 That thou mightest fear the LORD thy God, to keep all his statutes and his commandments, which I command thee, thou, and thy son, and thy son's son, all the days of thy life; and that thy days may be prolonged.

3 Hear therefore, O Israel, and observe to do *it;* that it may be well with thee, and that ye may increase mightily, as the LORD God of thy fathers hath promised thee, in the land that floweth with milk and honey.

4 Hear, O Israel: The LORD our God *is* one LORD:

5 And thou shalt love the LORD thy God with all thine heart, and with all thy soul, and with all thy might.

6 And these words, which I command thee this day, shall be in thine heart:

7 And thou shalt teach them diligently unto thy children, and shalt talk of them when thou sittest in thine house, and when thou walkest by the way, and when thou liest down, and when thou risest up.

8 And thou shalt bind them for a sign upon thine hand, and they shall be as frontlets between thine eyes.

9 And thou shalt write them upon the posts of thy house, and on thy gates.

10 And it shall be, when the LORD thy God shall have brought thee into the land which he sware unto thy fathers, to Abraham, to Isaac, and to Jacob, to give thee great and goodly cities, which thou buildedst not,

11 And houses full of all good *things,* which thou filledst not, and wells digged, which thou diggedst not, vineyards and olive trees, which thou plantedst not; when thou shalt have eaten and be full;

12 *Then* beware lest thou forget the LORD, which brought thee forth out of the land of Egypt, from the house of bondage.

13 Thou shalt fear the LORD thy God, and serve him, and shalt swear by his name.

14 Ye shall not go after other gods, of the gods of the people which *are* round about you;

15 (For the LORD thy God *is* a jealous God among you;) lest the anger of the LORD thy God be kindled against thee, and destroy thee from off the face of the earth.

The ultimate purpose of life is to love God with our whole being.

THE HIGHEST PURPOSE OF MAN

The older I grow—and I now stand on the brink of eternity—the more comes back to me that sentence in the Catechism which I learned when a child, and the fuller and deeper its meaning becomes: "What is the chief end of man? To glorify God and enjoy him forever."

—*Thomas Carlyle*

There can be no doubt in any man's mind nor in any man's heart that God is our sustenance and our strength. Each of us must believe wholeheartedly and fiercely in the power and the glory and the strength of God. Thus, it would be more proper to say that each man must seek the companionship of God. God awaits each one of us.

—*Harold K. Johnson*

Have courage for the great sorrow of life and patience for the smaller ones; and when you have laboriously accomplished your daily task, go to sleep in peace. God is awake.

—*Victor Hugo*

Let us have trust in God and comfort ourselves with the thought that all is well, if it happens according to the will of the Almighty, since He knows best what is good for our temporal as well as our eternal happiness and salvation.

—*Wolfgang Mozart*

The contemplation of celestial things will make a man both speak and think more sublimely and magnificently when he comes down to human affairs.

—*Cicero*

It is not difficult to see one vital significance of Jesus Christ: He has given us the most glorious interpretation of life's meaning that the sons of men have ever had. The fatherhood of God, the friendship of the Spirit, the sovereignty of righteousness, the law of love, and glory of service, the coming of the kingdom, the eternal hope—there never was an interpretation of life to compare with that.

—*Harry Emerson Fosdick*

Psalms

1 I will love thee, O Lord, my strength.

2 The Lord *is* my rock, and my fortress, and my deliverer; my God, my strength, in whom I will trust; my buckler, and the horn of my salvation, *and* my high tower.

3 I will call upon the Lord, *who is worthy* to be praised: so shall I be saved from mine enemies.

4 The sorrows of death compassed me, and the floods of ungodly men made me afraid.

5 The sorrows of hell compassed me about: the snares of death prevented me.

6 In my distress I called upon the Lord, and cried unto my God: he heard my voice out of his temple, and my cry came before him, *even* into his ears.

7 Then the earth shook and trembled; the foundations also of the hills moved and were shaken, because he was wroth.

16 He sent from above, he took me, he drew me out of many waters.

17 He delivered me from my strong enemy, and from them which hated me: for they were too strong for me.

18 They prevented me in the day of my calamity: but the Lord was my stay.

19 He brought me forth also into a large place; he delivered me, because he delighted in me.

20 The Lord rewarded me according to my righteousness; according to the cleanness of my hands hath he recompensed me.

21 For I have kept the ways of the Lord, and have not wickedly departed from my God.

22 For all his judgments *were* before me, and I did not put away his statutes from me.

23 I was also upright before him, and I kept myself from mine iniquity.

24 Therefore hath the Lord recompensed me according to my righteousness, according to the cleanness of my hands in his eyesight.

25 With the merciful thou wilt show thyself merciful; with an upright man thou wilt show thyself upright;

26 With the pure thou wilt shew thyself pure; and with the froward thou wilt shew thyself froward.

27 For thou wilt save the afflicted people; but wilt bring down high looks.

28 For thou wilt light my candle: the Lord my God will enlighten my darkness.

29 For by thee I have run through a troop; and by my God have I leaped over a wall.

30 *As for* God, his way *is* perfect: the word of the Lord is tried: he *is* a buckler to all those that trust in him.

31 For who *is* God save the Lord? or who *is* a rock save our God?

32 *It is* God that girdeth me with strength, and maketh my way perfect.

Love the Lord. He is everything.

He who leaves God out of his reasoning does not know how to count.

—Unknown

I fear God, and next to God I chiefly fear him who fears Him not.

—Saadia ben Joseph

All virtue consists in having a willing heart. God will lead you by the hand, if only you do not doubt, and are filled with love for Him rather than fear for yourself.

—Francois Fénelon

He hath shewed thee, O man, what is good; and what doth the Lord require of thee, but to do justly, and to love mercy, and to walk humbly with thy God?

—Micah 6:8

The science to which I pinned my faith is bankrupt. . . . Its counsels which should have established the millennium led directly to the suicide of Europe. I believed them once. . . . In their name I helped to destroy the faith of millions of worshipers in the temples of a thousand creeds. And now they look at me and witness the great tragedy of an atheist who has lost his faith.

—George Bernard Shaw

Even every one that is called by my name: for I have created him for my glory, I have formed him; yea, I have made him.

—Isaiah 43:7

Ecclesiastes

1 Remember now thy Creator in the days of thy youth, while the evil days come not, nor the years draw nigh, when thou shalt say, I have no pleasure in them;

2 While the sun, or the light, or the moon, or the stars, be not darkened, nor the clouds return after the rain:

3 In the day when the keepers of the house shall tremble, and the strong men shall bow themselves, and the grinders cease because they are few, and those that look out of the windows be darkened,

4 And the doors shall be shut in the streets, when the sound of the grinding is low, and he shall rise up at the voice of the bird, and all the daughters of music shall be brought low;

5 Also *when* they shall be afraid of *that which is* high, and fears *shall be* in the way, and the almond tree shall flourish, and the grasshopper shall be a burden, and desire shall fail: because man goeth to his long home, and the mourners go about the streets:

6 Or ever the silver cord be loosed, or the golden bowl be broken, or the pitcher be broken at the fountain, or the wheel broken at the cistern.

7 Then shall the dust return to the earth as it was: and the spirit shall return unto God who gave it.

8 Vanity of vanities, saith the Preacher; all *is* vanity.

9 And moreover, because the Preacher was wise, he still taught the people knowledge; yea, he gave good heed, and sought out, *and* set in order many proverbs.

10 The Preacher sought to find out acceptable words: and *that which was* written *was* upright, *even* words of truth.

11 The words of the wise *are* as goads, and as nails fastened *by* the masters of assemblies, *which* are given from one shepherd.

12 And further, by these, my son, be admonished: of making many books *there is* no end; and much study *is* a weariness of the flesh.

13 Let us hear the conclusion of the whole matter: Fear God, and keep his commandments: for this *is* the whole *duty* of man.

14 For God shall bring every work into judgment, with every secret thing, whether *it be* good, or whether *it be* evil.

Love God and do what He says.

Fear not that your life shall come to an end, but rather that it shall never have a beginning.

—*John Henry Newman*

I will place no value on anything I may possess except in relation to the kingdom of Christ. If anything I have will advance the interests of that kingdom, it shall be given away or kept, only as by giving or keeping it, I may promote the glory of Him to whom I owe all my hopes in time and eternity.

—*David Livingstone*

The final estimate of men shows that history cares not an iota for the rank or title a man has borne, or the office he has held, but only the quality of his deeds and the character of his mind and heart.

—*Samuel Brengle*

God never gave me a thing to do concerning which it were irreverent to ponder how the Son of God would have it.

—*George Macdonald*

The highest service may be prepared and done in the humblest surroundings. In silence, in waiting, in obscure, unnoticed offices, in years of uneventful, unrecorded duties, the Son of God grew and waxed strong.

—*Inscription in the*
Stanford University Chapel

I hold the precepts of Jesus as delivered by Himself, to be the most pure, benevolent, and sublime which have ever been preached to man. I adhere to the principles of the first age.

—*Thomas Jefferson*

Matthew

1 And seeing the multitudes, he went up into a mountain: and when he was set, his disciples came unto him:

2 And he opened his mouth, and taught them, saying,

3 Blessed *are* the poor in spirit: for theirs is the kingdom of heaven.

4 Blessed *are* they that mourn: for they shall be comforted.

5 Blessed *are* the meek: for they shall inherit the earth.

6 Blessed *are* they which do hunger and thirst after righteousness: for they shall be filled.

7 Blessed *are* the merciful: for they shall obtain mercy.

8 Blessed *are* the pure in heart: for they shall see God.

9 Blessed *are* the peacemakers: for they shall be called the children of God.

10 Blessed *are* they which are persecuted for righteousness' sake: for theirs is the kingdom of heaven.

11 Blessed are ye, when *men* shall revile you, and persecute *you,* and shall say all manner of evil against you falsely, for my sake.

12 Rejoice, and be exceeding glad: for great *is* your reward in heaven: for so persecuted they the prophets which were before you.

13 Ye are the salt of the earth: but if the salt have lost his savor, wherewith shall it be salted? it is thenceforth good for nothing, but to be cast out, and to be trodden under foot of men.

14 Ye are the light of the world. A city that is set on a hill cannot be hid.

15 Neither do men light a candle, and put it under a bushel, but on a candlestick; and it giveth light unto all that are in the house.

16 Let your light so shine before men, that they may see your good works, and glorify your Father which is in heaven.

17 Think not that I am come to destroy the law, or the prophets: I am not come to destroy, but to fulfil.

18 For verily I say unto you, Till heaven and earth pass, one jot or one tittle shall in no wise pass from the law, till all be fulfilled.

19 Whosoever therefore shall break one of these least commandments, and shall teach men so, he shall be called the least in the kingdom of heaven: but whosoever shall do and teach *them,* the same shall be called great in the kingdom of heaven.

20 For I say unto you, That except your righteousness shall exceed *the righteousness* of the scribes and Pharisees, ye shall in no case enter into the kingdom of heaven.

Follow Jesus Christ and you will be an able guide.

The peace of any man's soul who has out-grown mere self-indulgence can only come by going forward—on the deepest principles and final causes of things. Put God underneath all your life, and your life must rest upon the everlasting arms.

—Phillips Brooks

You cannot have faith and tension at the same time.

—Mahatma Gandhi

He who is convinced that there is naught for him to do but to enjoy himself is little more than an erect animal.

—J. Leonard Levy

Our cares we can cast on Thee, for Thou carest for us. How can we be troubled about the future road, since it belongs to Thee? How can we be troubled where it leads, since it finally but leads us to Thee!

—John Henry Newman

One's destiny is determined, not by what he possesses, but by what possesses him.

—Unknown

The crosses which we make for ourselves by a restless anxiety as to the future are not the crosses which come from God.

—Francois Fénelon

Loyalty that will do anything, that will endure anything, that will make the whole being consecrate to Him, is what Christ wants. Anything else is not worthy of Him.

—Burdett Hart

Who hath God hath all; who hath Him not hath less than nothing.

—Unknown

Matthew

25 Therefore I say unto you, Take no thought for your life, what ye shall eat, or what ye shall drink; nor yet for your body, what ye shall put on. Is not the life more than meat, and the body than raiment?

26 Behold the fowls of the air: for they sow not, neither do they reap, nor gather into barns; yet your heavenly Father feedeth them. Are ye not much better than they?

28 And why take ye thought for raiment? Consider the lilies of the field, how they grow; they toil not, neither do they spin:

29 And yet I say unto you, That even Solomon in all his glory was not arrayed like one of these.

30 Wherefore, if God so clothe the grass of the field, which to-day is, and to-morrow is cast into the oven, *shall he* not much more *clothe* you, O ye of little faith?

33 But seek ye first the kingdom of God, and his righteousness; and all these things shall be added unto you.

34 Take therefore no thought for the morrow: for the morrow shall take thought for the things of itself. Sufficient unto the day *is* the evil thereof.

CHAPTER 7

15 Beware of false prophets, which come to you in sheep's clothing, but inwardly they are ravening wolves.

16 Ye shall know them by their fruits. Do men gather grapes of thorns, or figs of thistles?

18 A good tree cannot bring forth evil fruit, neither *can* a corrupt tree bring forth good fruit.

20 Wherefore by their fruits ye shall know them.

22 Many will say to me in that day, Lord, Lord, have we not prophesied in thy name? and in thy name have cast out devils? and in thy name done many wonderful works?

23 And then will I profess unto them, I never knew you: depart from me, ye that work iniquity.

24 Therefore whosoever heareth these sayings of mine, and doeth them, I will liken him unto a wise man, which built his house upon a rock:

25 And the rain descended, and the floods came, and the winds blew, and beat upon that house; and it fell not: for it was founded upon a rock.

26 And every one that heareth these sayings of mine, and doeth them not, shall be likened unto a foolish man, which built his house upon the sand:

27 And the rain descended, and the floods came, and the winds blew, and beat upon that house; and it fell: and great was the fall of it.

28 And it came to pass, when Jesus had ended these sayings, the people were astonished at his doctrine:

29 For he taught them as *one* having authority, and not as the scribes.

What are you seeking first?

So long as we love we serve; so long as we are loved by others, I should say we are almost indispensable; and no man is useless while he has a friend.

—Robert Louis Stevenson

Teach us, good Lord,
    to give and not to count the cost,
    to toil and not to seek for rest
    to labor and not to ask for any reward
    save that of knowing that we do Thy will.

—Ignatius of Loyola

So this is now the mark by which we all shall certainly know whether the birth of the Lord Jesus is effective in us: if we take upon ourselves the needs of our neighbor.

—Martin Luther

On being asked by a Jewish lawyer which was the great commandment in the law, our Savior answered: "Thou shalt love the Lord thy God with all thy heart, and with all thy soul, and with all thy mind. This is the first and great commandment. And the second is like unto it; Thou shalt love thy neighbor as thyself. On these two commandments hang all the law and the prophets." It is manifest, therefore, that the love of God and the love of man are enjoined by the law; and as the genuine love of the one comprehends that of the other, the apostle assures us that "Love is the fulfilling of the law."

—John Jay

The measure of a man's humanity is the extent and intensity of his love for mankind.

—Ashley Montagu

If you neglect your love to your neighbor, in vain you profess your love to God; for by your love to God, the love to your neighbor is begotten, and by the love to your neighbor, your love to God is nourished.

—Francis Quarles

Luke

25 And, behold, a certain lawyer stood up, and tempted him, saying, Master, what shall I do to inherit eternal life?

26 He said unto him, What is written in the law? how readest thou?

27 And he answering said, Thou shalt love the Lord thy God with all thy heart, and with all thy soul, and with all thy strength, and with all thy mind; and thy neighbour as thyself.

28 And he said unto him, Thou hast answered right: this do, and thou shalt live.

29 But he, willing to justify himself, said unto Jesus, And who is my neighbour?

30 And Jesus answering said, A certain man went down from Jerusalem to Jericho, and fell among thieves, which stripped him of his raiment, and wounded *him,* and departed, leaving *him* half dead.

31 And by chance there came down a certain priest that way: and when he saw him, he passed by on the other side.

32 And likewise a Levite, when he was at the place, came and looked *on him,* and passed by on the other side.

33 But a certain Samaritan, as he journeyed, came where he was: and when he saw him, he had compassion *on him,*

34 And went *to him,* and bound up his wounds, pouring in oil and wine, and set him on his own beast, and brought him to an inn, and took care of him.

35 And on the morrow when he departed, he took out two pence, and gave *them* to the host, and said unto him, Take care of him; and whatsoever thou spendest more, when I come again, I will repay thee.

36 Which now of these three, thinkest thou, was neighbour unto him that fell among the thieves?

37 And he said, He that shewed mercy on him. Then said Jesus unto him, Go and do thou likewise.

38 Now it came to pass, as they went, that he entered into a certain village: and a certain woman named Martha received him into her house.

39 And she had a sister called Mary, which also sat at Jesus' feet, and heard his word.

40 But Martha was cumbered about much serving, and came to him, and said, Lord, dost thou not care that my sister hath left me to serve alone? bid her therefore that she help me.

41 And Jesus answered and said unto her, Martha, Martha, thou art careful and troubled about many things:

42 But one thing is needful; and Mary hath chosen that good part, which shall not be taken away from her.

***Your love for others is proof to yourself
that you love God.***

To believe only possibilities is not faith, but mere philosophy.

—Thomas Browne

If your faith in God is stronger for every humble task in which you need and get His aid, then that humble task is necessary to the fullness of your faith in God. It will make the music of your life more firm and solid.

—Phillips Brooks

If a man is not made for God, why is he happy only in God? If man is made for God, why is he opposed to God?

—Blaise Pascal

If you ask me how I believe in God, how God creates Himself in me, and reveals Himself to me, my answer may perhaps provoke your smiles or laughter, and even scandalize you. I believe in God as I believe in my friends, because I feel the breath of His affection, feel His invisible and tangible hand drawing me, leading me, grasping me.

—Miguel de Unamuno

My advice to you is, take a house next door to the Physician, for it will be very singular if you should prove to be the very first He ever turned away unhealed.

—Samuel Rutherford

The fact of Christ does not indeed show us everything, but it shows us the one thing we need to know—the character of God. God is the God who sent Jesus.

—P. Carnegie Simpson

God often visits us, but most of the time we are not at home.

—Joseph Roux

John

15 When Jesus therefore perceived that they would come and take him by force, to make him a king, he departed again into a mountain himself alone.

16 And when even was *now* come, his disciples went down unto the sea,

17 And entered into a ship, and went over the sea toward Capernaum. And it was now dark, and Jesus was not come to them.

18 And the sea arose by reason of a great wind that blew.

19 So when they had rowed about five and twenty or thirty furlongs, they see Jesus walking on the sea, and drawing nigh unto the ship: and they were afraid.

20 But he saith unto them, It is I; be not afraid.

21 Then they willingly received him into the ship: and immediately the ship was at the land whither they went.

24 When the people therefore saw that Jesus was not there, neither his disciples, they also took shipping, and came to Capernaum, seeking for Jesus.

25 And when they had found him on the other side of the sea, they said unto him, Rabbi, when camest thou hither?

26 Jesus answered them and said, Verily, verily, I say unto you, Ye seek me, not because ye saw the miracles, but because ye did eat of the loaves, and were filled.

27 Labor not for the meat which perisheth, but for that meat which endureth unto everlasting life, which the Son of man shall give unto you: for him hath God the Father sealed.

28 Then said they unto him, What shall we do, that we might work the works of God?

29 Jesus answered and said unto them, This is the work of God, that ye believe on him whom he hath sent.

30 They said therefore unto him, What sign showest thou then, that we may see, and believe thee? what dost thou work?

31 Our fathers did eat manna in the desert; as it is written, He gave them bread from heaven to eat.

32 Then Jesus said unto them, Verily, verily, I say unto you, Moses gave you not that bread from heaven; but my Father giveth you the true bread from heaven.

33 For the bread of God is he which cometh down from heaven, and giveth life unto the world.

34 Then said they unto him, Lord, evermore give us this bread.

35 And Jesus said unto them, I am the bread of life: he that cometh to me shall never hunger; and he that believeth on me shall never thirst.

40 And this is the will of him that sent me, that every one which seeth the Son, and believeth on him, may have everlasting life: and I will raise him up at the last day.

You do the work of God when you believe in Jesus Christ.

Not failure, but low aim, is crime.

—James Russell Lowell

Do not pray for easy lives! Pray to be stronger men. Do not pray for tasks equal to your powers. Pray for power equal to your tasks. Then the doing of your work shall be no miracle. But you shall be a miracle. Every day you shall wonder at yourself, at the richness of life which has come to you by the grace of God.

—Phillips Brooks

The strength of a man's virtue should not be measured by his special exertions, but by his habitual acts.

—Blaise Pascal

Thou hast made us, O Lord, for Thyself and our heart shall find no rest till it rest in Thee.

—Augustine

Christ is the center of all, and the goal to which all tends.

—Blaise Pascal

Tis not the dying for a faith that's so hard . . . tis the living up to it that's difficult.

—William Makepeace Thackeray

The true worth of a man is to be measured by the objects he pursues.

—Marcus Aurelius

Jesus Christ and His precepts are found to hit the moral experience of mankind; to hit it in the critical points; to hit it lastingly; and when doubts are thrown upon their really hitting it, then to come out stronger than ever.

—Matthew Arnold

Philippians

1 Finally, my brethren, rejoice in the Lord. To write the same things to you, to me indeed *is* not grievous, but for you *it is* safe.

2 Beware of dogs, beware of evil workers, beware of the concision.

3 For we are the circumcision, which worship God in the spirit, and rejoice in Christ Jesus, and have no confidence in the flesh.

4 Though I might also have confidence in the flesh. If any other man thinketh that he hath whereof he might trust in the flesh, I more:

5 Circumcised the eighth day, of the stock of Israel, *of* the tribe of Benjamin, a Hebrew of the Hebrews; as touching the law, a Pharisee;

6 Concerning zeal, persecuting the church; touching the righteousness which is in the law, blameless.

7 But what things were gain to me, those I counted loss for Christ.

8 Yea doubtless, and I count all things *but* loss for the excellency of the knowledge of Christ Jesus my Lord: for whom I have suffered the loss of all things, and do count them *but* dung, that I may win Christ,

9 And be found in him, not having mine own righteousness, which is of the law, but that which is through the faith of Christ, the righteousness which is of God by faith:

10 That I may know him, and the power of his resurrection, and the fellowship of his sufferings, being made conformable unto his death;

11 If by any means I might attain unto the resurrection of the dead.

12 Not, as though I had already attained, either were already perfect. . . .

13 Brethren, I count not myself to have apprehended: but *this* one thing *I do,* forgetting those things which are behind, and reaching forth unto those things which are before,

14 I press toward the mark for the prize of the high calling of God in Christ Jesus.

17 Brethren, be followers together of me, and mark them which walk so as ye have us for an ensample.

18 (For many walk, of whom I have told you often, and now tell you even weeping, *that they are* the enemies of the cross of Christ:

19 Whose end *is* destruction, whose God *is their* belly, and *whose* glory *is* in their shame, who mind earthly things.)

20 For our conversation is in heaven; from whence also we look for the Saviour, the Lord Jesus Christ:

21 Who shall change our vile body, that it may be fashioned like unto his glorious body, according to the working whereby he is able even to subdue all things unto himself.

The goal of life: to know Jesus Christ.

Reflections

God's Everything — Jesus Christ

The death of Socrates, peacefully philosophizing among friends, appears the most agreeable that one could wish: that of Jesus, expiring in agonies, abused, insulted, and accused by a whole nation, is the most horrible that one could fear. Yes, if the life and death of Socrates were those of a sage, the life and death of Jesus are those of a God.

—Jean Jacques Rousseau

It is a terrible mistake to understand Jesus as having been crucified by some especially bad people in the first century. Jesus was crucified by the highest reach of human religiosity, morality, and political justice.

—Albert T. Mollegen

To have faith in the crucified One means to permit oneself to be crucified with Him, to permit this judgment also to be passed against oneself.

—Rudolph Bultmann

No man can know his true self, caught between this potential for depravity and this potential for divinity, except in the light of what happened on Calvary.

—Stuart LeRoy Anderson

The nail-pierced Figure on Calvary haunts our race as a symbol of what is forever taking place generation after generation, and of what each of us has his part in.

—Henry Sloane Coffin

Not only do we not know God save through Jesus Christ, but we do not know ourselves save through Jesus Christ. We know neither life nor death save through Jesus Christ. Apart from Jesus Christ we know not what our life is, nor our death, nor God, nor ourselves.

—Blaise Pascal

Isaiah

1 Who hath believed our report? and to whom is the arm of the Lord revealed?

2 For he shall grow up before him as a tender plant, and as a root out of a dry ground: he hath no form nor comeliness; and when we shall see him, *there is* no beauty that we should desire him.

3 He is despised and rejected of men; a man of sorrows, and acquainted with grief: and we hid as it were *our* faces from him; he was despised, and we esteemed him not.

4 Surely he hath borne our griefs, and carried our sorrows: yet we did esteem him stricken, smitten of God, and afflicted.

5 But he *was* wounded for our transgressions, *he was* bruised for our iniquities: the chastisement of our peace *was* upon him; and with his stripes we are healed.

6 All we like sheep have gone astray; we have turned every one to his own way; and the Lord hath laid on him the iniquity of us all.

7 He was oppressed, and he was afflicted, yet he opened not his mouth: he is brought as a lamb to the slaughter, and as a sheep before her shearers is dumb, so he openeth not his mouth.

8 He was taken from prison and from judgment: and who shall declare his generation? for he was cut off out of the land of the living: for the transgression of my people was he stricken.

9 And he made his grave with the wicked, and with the rich in his death; because he had done no violence, neither *was any* deceit in his mouth.

10 Yet it pleased the Lord to bruise him; he hath put *him* to grief: when thou shalt make his soul an offering for sin, he shall see *his* seed, he shall prolong *his* days, and the pleasure of the Lord shall prosper in his hand.

11 He shall see of the travail of his soul, *and* shall be satisfied: by his knowledge shall my righteous servant justify many; for he shall bear their iniquities.

12 Therefore will I divide him *a portion* with the great, and he shall divide the spoil with the strong; because he hath poured out his soul unto death: and he was numbered with the transgressors; and he bare the sin of many, and made intercession for the transgressors.

Jesus Christ died that you might live.

No Cross, No Crown.

—Thomas Fuller

I have now disposed of all my property to my family. There is one thing more I wish I could give them and that is faith in Jesus Christ. If they had that and I had not given them one shilling, they would have been rich; and if they had not that, and I had given them all the world, they would be poor indeed.

—Patrick Henry

He is no fool who gives what he cannot keep to gain what he cannot lose.

—Jim Elliot

I am more convinced than I am of my own existence that the view of life Christ came into the world to preach, and died to sanctify, remains as true and valid as ever; and that all who care to may live thereby, finding an enlightenment and serenity not otherwise attainable.

—Malcolm Muggeridge

If Socrates would enter the room we should rise and do him honor. But if Jesus Christ came into the room we should fall down on our knees and worship Him.

—Napoléon Bonaparte

My memory is almost gone, but I remember one thing: that I am a great sinner and Christ is a great Savior.

—John Newton, author of
"Amazing Grace"

Matthew

13 When Jesus came into the coasts of Caesarea Philippi, he asked his disciples, saying, Whom do men say that I, the Son of man, am?

14 And they said, Some *say that thou art* John the Baptist; some, Elias; and others, Jeremias, or one of the prophets.

15 He saith unto them, But whom say ye that I am?

16 And Simon Peter answered and said, Thou art the Christ, the Son of the living God.

17 And Jesus answered and said unto him, Blessed art thou, Simon Barjona: for flesh and blood hath not revealed *it* unto thee, but my Father which is in heaven.

18 And I say also unto thee, That thou art Peter, and upon this rock I will build my church; and the gates of hell shall not prevail against it.

19 And I will give unto thee the keys of the kingdom of heaven: and whatsoever thou shalt bind on earth shall be bound in heaven; and whatsoever thou shalt loose on earth shall be loosed in heaven.

20 Then charged he his disciples that they should tell no man that he was Jesus the Christ.

21 From that time forth began Jesus to show unto his disciples, how that he must go unto Jerusalem, and suffer many things of the elders and chief priests and scribes, and be killed, and be raised again the third day.

22 Then Peter took him, and began to rebuke him, saying, Be it far from thee, Lord: this shall not be unto thee.

23 But he turned, and said unto Peter, Get thee behind me, Satan: thou art an offence unto me: for thou savourest not the things that be of God, but those that be of men.

24 Then said Jesus unto his disciples, If any man will come after me, let him deny himself, and take up his cross, and follow me.

25 For whosoever will save his life shall lose it: and whosoever will lose his life for my sake shall find it.

26 For what is a man profited, if he shall gain the whole world, and lose his own soul? or what shall a man give in exchange for his soul?

27 For the Son of man shall come in the glory of his Father with his angels; and then he shall reward every man according to his works.

Who do you think Jesus Christ is?

After reading the doctrine of Plato, Socrates, or Aristotle, we feel that the specific difference between their words and Christ's is the difference between an inquiry and a revelation.

—Joseph Parker

I am nothing, but truth is everything. I know I am right, because I know that liberty is right, for Christ teaches it, and Christ is God.

—Abraham Lincoln

The Sermon on the Mount was and is seditious. It finally put Jesus on the cross, and it will do the same for his followers who follow it in modern life.

—E. Stanley Jones

A chief event in life is the day in which we have encountered a mind that startled us.

—Ralph Waldo Emerson

He who shall introduce into public affairs the principles of Christ will change the face of the world.

—Benjamin Franklin

Is it any wonder that to this day this Galilean is too much for our small hearts?

—H. G. Wells

All we want in life, we shall find in Christ. If we want little, we shall find little. If we want much, we shall find much; but if, in utter helplessness, we cast our all on Christ, He will be to us the whole treasury of God.

—Henry Benjamin Whipple

Luke

25 And, behold, there was a man in Jerusalem, whose name *was* Simeon; and the same man *was* just and devout, waiting for the consolation of Israel: and the Holy Ghost was upon him.

26 And it was revealed unto him by the Holy Ghost, that he should not see death, before he had seen the Lord's Christ.

27 And he came by the Spirit into the temple: and when the parents brought in the child Jesus, to do for him after the custom of the law,

28 Then took he him up in his arms, and blessed God, and said,

29 Lord, now lettest thou thy servant depart in peace, according to thy word:

30 For mine eyes have seen thy salvation,

31 Which thou hast prepared before the face of all people;

32 A light to lighten the Gentiles, and the glory of thy people Israel.

33 And Joseph and his mother marveled at those things which were spoken of him.

34 And Simeon blessed them, and said unto Mary his mother, Behold, this *child* is set for the fall and rising again of many in Israel; and for a sign which shall be spoken against;

35 (Yea, a sword shall pierce through thy own soul also;) that the thoughts of many hearts may be revealed.

40 And the child grew, and waxed strong in spirit, filled with wisdom; and the grace of God was upon him.

41 Now his parents went to Jerusalem every year at the feast of the passover.

42 And when he was twelve years old, they went up to Jerusalem after the custom of the feast.

43 And when they had fulfilled the days, as they returned, the child Jesus tarried behind in Jerusalem; and Joseph and his mother knew not *of it.*

46 And it came to pass, that after three days they found him in the temple, sitting in the midst of the doctors, both hearing them, and asking them questions.

47 And all that heard him were astonished at his understanding and answers.

48 And when they saw him, they were amazed: and his mother said unto him, Son, why hast thou thus dealt with us? behold, thy father and I have sought thee sorrowing.

49 And he said unto them, How is it that ye sought me? wist ye not that I must be about my Father's business?

50 And they understood not the saying which he spake unto them.

51 And he went down with them, and came to Nazareth, and was subject unto them: but his mother kept all these sayings in her heart.

52 And Jesus increased in wisdom and stature, and in favor with God and man.

Men from every age have marveled at the life and teachings of Jesus Christ.

Blessed be His name for shining upon so dark a heart as mine.

—Oliver Cromwell

Jesus knew that He had come to kindle a fire on earth. . . . He saw that what was exalted among man was an abomination before God.

—Walter Rauschenbush

Jesus astonishes and overpowers sensual people. They cannot unite Him to history or reconcile Him with themselves.

—Ralph Waldo Emerson

In no one else in all history do you find an abiding hatred, an immortal hatred except against Our Lord. . . . The hatred against Christ has never weakened even after twenty centuries . . . because He is still an obstacle—an obstacle to sin, to selfishness, to godlessness, and to the spirit of the world.

—Fulton J. Sheen

There is no ill which may not be dissipated, like the dark, if you let in a stronger light upon it.

—Henry David Thoreau

I believe in Christ like I believe in the sun, not just because I see it, but because by it I can see everything else.

—C. S. Lewis

John

1 In the beginning was the Word, and the Word was with God, and the Word was God.

2 The same was in the beginning with God.

3 All things were made by him; and without him was not any thing made that was made.

4 In him was life; and the life was the light of men.

5 And the light shineth in darkness; and the darkness comprehended it not.

6 There was a man sent from God, whose name *was* John.

7 The same came for a witness, to bear witness of the Light, that all *men* through him might believe.

8 He was not that Light, but *was sent* to bear witness of that Light.

9 *That* was the true Light, which lighteth every man that cometh into the world.

10 He was in the world, and the world was made by him, and the world knew him not.

11 He came unto his own, and his own received him not.

12 But as many as received him, to them gave he power to become the sons of God, *even* to them that believe on his name:

13 Which were born, not of blood, nor of the will of the flesh, nor of the will of man, but of God.

14 And the Word was made flesh, and dwelt among us, (and we beheld his glory, the glory as of the only begotten of the Father,) full of grace and truth.

15 John bare witness of him, and cried, saying, This was he of whom I spake, He that cometh after me is preferred before me; for he was before me.

16 And of his fulness have all we received, and grace for grace.

17 For the law was given by Moses, *but* grace and truth came by Jesus Christ.

18 No man hath seen God at any time; the only begotten Son, which is in the bosom of the Father, he hath declared *him*.

Jesus Christ is the light of the world.

God forgives—forgives not capriciously, but with wise, definite, divine prearrangement; forgives universally, on the ground of an atonement and on the condition of repentance and faith.

—Richard Salter Storrs

We pardon in the degree that we love.

—Francois de la Rochefoucauld

He did not come to conquer by force of armies and physical weapons but by love planted in the hearts of individuals.

—W. W. Melton

It is scarcely possible that a misleading instinct would be planted in all men in all ages.

—O. P. Eaches

To follow Christ means to learn the art of life. And the whole curriculum lies in the words, "Learn of me."

—Unknown

The distinction between following Christ and all other systems of religion consists largely in this: that in these other, men are found seeking after God, while Christ is God seeking after men.

—Unknown

They that seek the Lord shall not want any good thing.

—Psalm 34:10

John

5 Then cometh he to a city of Samaria, which is called Sychar, near to the parcel of ground that Jacob gave to his son Joseph.

6 Now Jacob's well was there. Jesus therefore, being wearied with *his* journey, sat thus on the well: *and it* was about the sixth hour.

7 There cometh a woman of Samaria to draw water: Jesus saith unto her, Give me to drink.

8 (For his disciples were gone away unto the city to buy meat.)

9 Then saith the woman of Samaria unto him, How is it that thou, being a Jew, askest drink of me, which am a woman of Samaria? for the Jews have no dealings with the Samaritans.

10 Jesus answered and said unto her, If thou knewest the gift of God, and who it is that saith to thee, Give me to drink; thou wouldest have asked of him, and he would have given thee living water.

11 The woman saith unto him, Sir, thou hast nothing to draw with, and the well is deep: from whence then hast thou that living water?

12 Art thou greater than our father Jacob, which gave us the well, and drank thereof himself, and his children, and his cattle?

13 Jesus answered and said unto her, Whosoever drinketh of this water shall thirst again:

14 But whosoever drinketh of the water that I shall give him shall never thirst; but the water that I shall give him shall be in him a well of water springing up into everlasting life.

15 The woman saith unto him, Sir, give me this water, that I thirst not, neither come hither to draw.

16 Jesus saith unto her, Go, call thy husband, and come hither.

17 The woman answered and said, I have no husband. Jesus said unto her, Thou hast well said, I have no husband:

18 For thou hast had five husbands; and he whom thou now hast is not thy husband: in that saidst thou truly.

19 The woman saith unto him, Sir, I perceive that thou art a prophet.

20 Our fathers worshipped in this mountain; and ye say, that in Jerusalem is the place where men ought to worship.

21 Jesus saith unto her, Woman, believe me, the hour cometh, when ye shall neither in this mountain, nor yet at Jerusalem, worship the Father.

22 Ye worship ye know not what: we know what we worship; for salvation is of the Jews.

23 But the hour cometh, and now is, when the true worshippers shall worship the Father in spirit and in truth: for the Father seeketh such to worship him.

24 God *is* a Spirit: and they that worship him must worship *him* in spirit and in truth.

You never have to thirst again.

Joy has its springs deep down inside. And that spring never runs dry, no matter what happens. Only Jesus gives that joy. He had joy, singing its music within, even under the shadow of the cross. It is an unknown word and thing except as He has sway within.

—*Samuel Dickey Gordon*

... thou anointest my head with oil; my cup runneth over.

—*Psalm 23:5*

I believe that a personal relationship with the hero of the Bible, Jesus Christ, can provide the foundation for this life of purpose, for it is Christ who said, "I came that they may have and enjoy life, and have it in abundance—to the full, till it overflows."

—*Mark O. Hatfield*

Daniel A. Poling was once asked by a young man, "What do you know about God?" Dr. Poling answered, "Mighty little, but what I know has changed my entire life.

Glorious indeed is the world of God around us, but more glorious the world of God within us. There lies the land of song; there lies the poet's native land.

—*Henry Wadsworth Longfellow*

John

1 Verily, verily, I say unto you, He that entereth not by the door into the sheepfold, but climbeth up some other way, the same is a thief and a robber.

2 But he that entereth in by the door is the shepherd of the sheep.

6 This parable spake Jesus unto them; but they understood not what things they were which he spake unto them.

7 Then said Jesus unto them again, Verily, verily, I say unto you, I am the door of the sheep.

8 All that ever came before me are thieves and robbers: but the sheep did not hear them.

9 I am the door: by me if any man enter in, he shall be saved, and shall go in and out, and find pasture.

10 The thief cometh not, but for to steal, and to kill, and to destroy: I am come that they might have life, and that they might have *it* more abundantly.

11 I am the good shepherd: the good shepherd giveth his life for the sheep.

14 I am the good shepherd, and know my *sheep,* and am known of mine.

15 As the Father knoweth me, even so know I the Father: and I lay down my life for the sheep.

17 Therefore doth my Father love me, because I lay down my life, that I might take it again.

18 No man taketh it from me, but I lay it down of myself. I have power to lay it down, and I have power to take it again. This commandment have I received of my Father.

19 There was a division therefore again among the Jews for these sayings.

20 And many of them said, He hath a devil, and is mad; why hear ye him?

21 Others said, These are not the words of him that hath a devil. Can a devil open the eyes of the blind?

22 And it was at Jerusalem the feast of the dedication, and it was winter.

23 And Jesus walked in the temple in Solomon's porch.

24 Then came the Jews round about him, and said unto him, How long dost thou make us to doubt? If thou be the Christ, tell us plainly.

25 Jesus answered them, I told you, and ye believed not: the works that I do in my Father's name, they bear witness of me.

26 But ye believe not, because ye are not of my sheep, as I said unto you.

27 My sheep hear my voice, and I know them, and they follow me:

28 And I give unto them eternal life; and they shall never perish, neither shall any *man* pluck them out of my hand.

29 My Father, which gave *them* me, is greater than all; and no *man* is able to pluck *them* out of my Father's hand.

30 I and *my* Father are one.

Do you want life that is more abundant?

To him that overcometh will I grant to sit with me in my throne, even as I also overcame, and am set down with my Father in his throne.

—Revelation 3:21

To the believer in Christ death has redemptive significance. It is the portal through which we enter the presence of our Lord.

—Hilys Jasper

It is with men as with wheat: the light heads are erect even in the presence of Omnipotence, but the full heads bow in reverence before Him.

—Unknown

Is death the last sleep? No, it is the last and final awakening.

—Sir Walter Scott

It is simple dogmatism that would deny immortality on scientific grounds; at any rate, we have not the knowledge to take up such an attitude.

—Sir James Young Simpson

I am the resurrection and the life: he that believeth in me, though he were dead, yet shall he live.

—John 11:25

All the world's joy comes from the grave of our risen Lord.

—Unknown

John

1 The first *day* of the week cometh Mary Magadalene early, when it was yet dark, unto the sepulchre, and seeth the stone taken away from the sepulchre.

2 Then she runneth, and cometh to Simon Peter, and to the other disciple, whom Jesus loved, and saith unto them, They have taken away the Lord out of the sepulchre, and we know not where they have laid him.

4 So they ran both together: and the other disciple did outrun Peter, and came first to the sepulchre.

5 And he stooping down, *and looking in,* saw the linen clothes lying; yet went he not in.

6 Then cometh Simon Peter following him, and went into the sepulchre, and seeth the linen clothes lie,

7 And the napkin, that was about his head, not lying with the linen clothes, but wrapped together in a place by itself.

8 Then went in also that other disciple, which came first to the sepulchre, and he saw, and believed.

9 For as yet they knew not the Scripture, that he must rise again from the dead.

10 Then the disciples went away again unto their own home.

11 But Mary stood without at the sepulchre weeping: and as she wept, she stooped down, *and looked* into the sepulchre,

12 And seeth two angels in white sitting, the one at the head, and the other at the feet, where the body of Jesus had lain.

13 And they say unto her, Woman, why weepest thou? She saith unto them, Because they have taken away my Lord, and I know not where they have laid him.

14 And when she had thus said, she turned herself back, and saw Jesus standing, and knew not that it was Jesus.

15 Jesus saith unto her, Woman, why weepest thou? whom seekest thou? She, supposing him to be the gardener, saith unto him, Sir, if thou have borne him hence, tell me where thou hast laid him, and I will take him away.

16 Jesus saith unto her, Mary. She turned herself, and saith unto him, Rabboni: which is to say, Master.

19 Then the same day at evening, being the first *day* of the week, when the doors were shut where the disciples were assembled for fear of the Jews, came Jesus and stood in the midst, and saith unto them, Peace *be* unto you.

20 And when he had so said, he shewed unto them *his* hands and his side. Then were the disciples glad, when they saw the Lord.

21 Then said Jesus to them again, Peace *be* unto you: as *my* Father hath sent me, even so send I you.

Jesus Christ is risen!

There was one who thought he was above me, and he was above me until he had that thought.

—Elbert Hubbard

The true measure of a man is not the number of servants he has, but the number of people he serves.

—Arnold Glasgow

We are made for the splendor of celestial glory. If the Lord also reserves for us a little honor on earth, this is of no value at all and perishes quickly if it is not of God. If the Lord on the contrary, disposes that the value of our life be entirely hidden in Him it would be ridiculous to look for anything else.

—Pope John XXIII

One must reach the point of not caring two straws about his own status before he can wish wholly for God's kingdom, not his own, to be established.

—C. S. Lewis

Oh, how distressing it sometimes is to live with certain colleagues who always talk only of the outer forms of priestly activity, who find it hard to repress in their hearts the thirst and pursuit, not always veiled nor modest, for promotions, advancement, distinctions: and who are wont to interpret everything in a minor key, thereby preparing a premature, dreary, and irksome old age for themselves.

—Pope John XXIII

If any man will come after me, let him deny himself, and take up his cross, and follow me.

—Matthew 16:24

Philippians

1 If *there be* therefore any consolation in Christ, if any comfort of love, if any fellowship of the Spirit, if any bowels and mercies,

2 Fulfil ye my joy, that ye be likeminded, having the same love, *being* of one accord, of one mind.

3 *Let* nothing *be done* through strife or vainglory; but in lowliness of mind let each esteem other better than themselves.

4 Look not every man on his own things, but every man also on the things of others.

5 Let this mind be in you, which was also in Christ Jesus:

6 Who, being in the form of God, thought it not robbery to be equal with God:

7 But made himself of no reputation, and took upon him the form of a servant, and was made in the likeness of men:

8 And being found in fashion as a man, he humbled himself, and became obedient unto death, even the death of the cross.

9 Wherefore God also hath highly exalted him, and given him a name which is above every name:

10 That at the name of Jesus every knee should bow, of *things* in heaven, and *things* in earth, and *things* under the earth;

11 And *that* every tongue should confess that Jesus Christ *is* Lord, to the glory of God the Father.

12 Wherefore, my beloved, as ye have always obeyed, not as in my presence only, but now much more in my absence, work out your own salvation with fear and trembling:

13 For it is God which worketh in you both to will and to do of *his* good pleasure.

14 Do all things without murmurings and disputings:

15 That ye may be blameless and harmless, the sons of God, without rebuke, in the midst of a crooked and perverse nation, among whom ye shine as lights in the world;

16 Holding forth the word of life; that I may rejoice in the day of Christ, that I have not run in vain, neither labored in vain.

Jesus Christ is the standard of true greatness.

The ascension has not taken Him away from you, but it has carried you up to Him.

—Unknown

The very helplessness of the world today is in itself a repudiation of that self-sufficient and self-confident view of life that the world in its progressive development has outgrown the need of Christ. It is following Christ that gives the world what it most needs—a standard of right living, a cause to maintain and defend, a Leader to follow, and a law to obey.

—Unknown

The need is clear and the time is ripe for a genuine spiritual reformation in leaders of nations if life is to endure on this planet, take on greater quality and meaning, and be worthy of the sacrifice and example of the Jesus Christ we worship.

—Henry H. Fowler

"Jesus." It was the voice of one of the robbers.
"Jesus," he says painfully, "remember me, when thou comest into thy kingdom."   Read that, oh men, and bow your heads. You who have let yourself picture Him as weak, as a Man of sorrows, uninspiring, glad to die. There have been leaders who could call forth enthusiasm when their fortunes ran high. But He, when His enemies had done their worst, so bore Himself that a crucified felon looked into His dying eyes and saluted him as King.

—Bruce Barton

A man who puts aside his trust in Christ because he is going into society is like one taking off his shoes because he is about to walk upon thorns.

—Unknown

Christ is the only transforming power there is and we strive in vain without Him whether we are building a life or a country.

—Rosalie Mills Appleby

Colossians

9 For this cause we also, since the day we heard *it,* do not cease to pray for you, and to desire that ye might be filled with the knowledge of his will in all wisdom and spiritual understanding;

10 That ye might walk worthy of the Lord unto all pleasing, being fruitful in every good work, and increasing in the knowledge of God;

13 Who hath delivered us from the power of darkness, and hath translated *us* into the kingdom of his dear Son:

20 And, having made peace through the blood of his cross, by him to reconcile all things unto himself; by him, *I say,* whether *they be* things in earth, or things in heaven.

21 And you, that were sometime alienated and enemies in *your* mind by wicked works, yet now hath he reconciled. . . .

26 *Even* the mystery which hath been hid from ages and from generations, but now is made manifest to his saints:

27 To whom God would make known what *is* the riches of the glory of this mystery among the Gentiles; which is Christ in you, the hope of glory:

28 Whom we preach, warning every man, and teaching every man in all wisdom; that we may present every man perfect in Christ Jesus:

29 Whereunto I also labour, striving according to his working, which worketh in me mightily.

CHAPTER 2

1 For I would that ye knew what great conflict I have for you, and *for* them at Laodicea, and *for* as many as have not seen my face in the flesh;

2 That their hearts might be comforted, being knit together in love, and unto all riches of the full assurance of understanding, to the acknowledgment of the mystery of God, and of the Father, and of Christ;

3 In whom are hid all the treasures of wisdom and knowledge.

4 And this I say, lest any man should beguile you with enticing words.

5 For though I be absent in the flesh, yet am I with you in the spirit, joying and beholding your order, and the steadfastness of your faith in Christ.

6 As ye have therefore received Christ Jesus the Lord, *so* walk ye in him:

7 Rooted and built up in him, and stablished in the faith, as ye have been taught, abounding therein with thanksgiving.

8 Beware lest any man spoil you through philosophy and vain deceit after the tradition of men, after the rudiments of the world, and not after Christ.

9 For in him dwelleth all the fulness of the Godhead bodily.

10 And ye are complete in him, which is the head of all principality and power:

God's secret plan for the nations—Christ in you.

In the evening I went very unwillingly to a society in Aldersgate Street, where one was reading Luther's preface to the Epistle to the Romans. About a quarter before nine, while he was describing the change which God works in the heart through faith in Christ, I felt my heart strangely warmed. I felt I did trust in Christ, Christ alone for salvation; and an assurance was given me that He had taken away my sins, even mine, and saved me from the law of sin and death.

—John Wesley

Lincoln said, "When I went to Gettysburg I then and there consecrated myself to Christ." Something happened to Lincoln at Gettysburg. Something could happen to you to change your life and make you the kind of man the world needs at this hour of history.

—Unknown

There is a God-created vacuum in the heart of every man, which cannot be satisfied by any created thing, but only by God the Creator, made known through Jesus Christ.

—Blaise Pascal

The heart of the whole matter is faith in Jesus Christ. Do we believe in Him as passionately as others believe in their own ideas and systems? If we do, then we ought to do better than they, for we worship a person; they worship an idea. We worship life and strength and love and victory; they worship negation and hatred. Christ can do without us—and He may be doing so already in the vast spaces of Asia and Africa— and if we fail Him, it cannot be that He failed us; we will only have proven that we are unprofitable servants.

—Charles Malik

John

1 Whosoever believeth that Jesus is the Christ is born of God. . . .

2 By this we know that we love the children of God, when we love God, and keep his commandments.

3 For this is the love of God, that we keep his commandments: and his commandments are not grievous.

5 Who is he that overcometh the world, but he that believeth that Jesus is the Son of God?

6 This is he that came by water and blood, *even* Jesus Christ; not by water only, but by water and blood. And it is the Spirit that beareth witness, because the Spirit is truth.

7 For there are three that bear record in heaven, the Father, the Word, and the Holy Ghost: and these three are one.

8 And there are three that bear witness in earth, the spirit, and the water, and the blood: and these three agree in one.

9 If we receive the witness of men, the witness of God is greater: for this is the witness of God which he hath testified of his Son.

10 He that believeth on the Son of God hath the witness in himself: he that believeth not God hath made him a liar; because he believeth not the record that God gave of his Son.

11 And this is the record, that God hath given to us eternal life, and this life is in his Son.

12 He that hath the Son hath life; *and* he that hath not the Son of God hath not life.

13 These things have I written unto you that believe on the name of the Son of God; that ye may know that ye have eternal life, and that ye may believe on the name of the Son of God.

14 And this is the confidence that we have in him, that, if we ask any thing according to his will, he heareth us:

15 And if we know that he hear us, whatsoever we ask, we know that we have the petitions that we desired of him.

16 If any man see his brother sin a sin *which is* not unto death, he shall ask, and he shall give him life for them that sin not unto death. There is a sin unto death: I do not say that he shall pray for it.

17 All unrighteousness is sin: and there is a sin not unto death.

18 We know that whosoever is born of God sinneth not; but he that is begotten of God keepeth himself, and that wicked one toucheth him not.

19 *And* we know that we are of God, and the whole world lieth in wickedness.

20 And we know that the Son of God is come, and hath given us an understanding, that we may know him that is true, and we are in him that is true, *even* in his Son Jesus Christ. This is the true God, and eternal life.

21 Little children, keep yourselves from idols. Amen.

Jesus Christ is the secret of man's renewal, both personal and global.

Reflections

God's Spirit—
The Holy Spirit

We have substituted relativity for reality, psychology for prayer, an inferiority complex for sin, social control for family worship, autosuggestion for conversion, reflex action for revelation, the spirit of the wheels for the power of the Spirit.

—Hugh Thomson Kerr

The Spirit of God first imparts love; He next inspires hope, and then gives liberty; and that is about the last thing we have in many of our churches.

—Dwight L. Moody

Every time we say, "I believe in the Holy Spirit," we mean that we believe that there is a living God able and willing to enter human personality and change it.

—J. B. Phillips

Not by might, nor by power, but by my spirit, saith the Lord of hosts.

—Zechariah 4:6

All our natural powers can be used mightily by God, but only when we think nothing of them and surrender ourselves to be simply the vehicles of divine power, letting God use us as He wills, content to be even despised by men if He be glorified.

—G. H. Knight

He that believeth on me, as the scripture hath said, out of his belly shall flow rivers of living water. (But this spake he of the Spirit, which they that believe on him should receive. . . .)

—John 7:38,39

Isaiah

10 Behold, the Lord GOD will come with strong *hand,* and his arm shall rule for him: behold, his reward *is* with him, and his work before him.

11 He shall feed his flock like a shepherd: he shall gather the lambs with his arm, and carry *them* in his bosom, *and* shall gently lead ·those that are with young.

12 Who hath measured the waters in the hollow of his hand, and meted out heaven with the span, and comprehended the dust of the earth in a measure, and weighed the mountains in scales, and the hills in a balance?

13 Who hath directed the Spirit of the LORD, or *being* his counselor hath taught him?

14 With whom took he counsel, and *who* instructed him, and taught him in the path of judgment, and taught him knowledge, and showed to him the way of understanding?

17 All nations before him *are* as nothing; and they are counted to him less than nothing, and vanity.

18 To whom then will ye liken God? or what likeness will ye compare unto him?

21 Have ye not known? have ye not heard? hath it not been told you from the beginning? have ye not understood from the foundations of the earth?

22 *It* is he that sitteth upon the circle of the earth, and the inhabitants thereof *are* as grasshoppers; that stretcheth out the heavens as a curtain, and spreadeth them out as a tent to dwell in:

23 That bringeth the princess to nothing; he maketh the judges of the earth as vanity.

24 Yea, they shall not be planted; yea, they shall not be sown; yea, their stock shall not take root in the earth: and he shall also blow upon them, and they shall wither, and the whirlwind shall take them away as stubble.

25 To whom then will ye liken me, or shall I be equal? saith the Holy One.

26 Lift up your eyes on high, and behold who hath created these *things,* that bringeth out their host by number: he called them all by names by the greatness of his might, for that *he is* strong in power; not one faileth.

28 Hast thou not known? hast thou not heard, *that* the everlasting God, the LORD, the Creator of the ends of the earth, fainteth not, neither is weary? *there* is no searching of his understanding.

29 He giveth power to the faint; and to *them that have* no might he increaseth strength.

30 Even the youths shall faint and be weary, and the young men shall utterly fall:

31 But they that wait upon the LORD shall renew *their* strength; they shall mount up with wings as eagles; they shall run, and not be weary; *and* they shall walk, and not faint.

Be strong in the Lord and in His power.

There dwelt in Him a Spirit great and universal, as that of the round world itself, compact of law and truth, a Spirit greater than the world, conveying life and vision from the source from which all worlds and existence itself must have taken origin. He is our revelation. In Him is our life explained and our knowledge made comprehensible . . . in Him we are made known to ourselves—in Him because He is God.

—*Woodrow Wilson*

We must not be content to be cleansed from sin; we must be filled with the Spirit.

—*John Fletcher*

Even those who have renounced Christ's way and attack it, in their inmost being still follow Christ's ideals, for hitherto neither their subtlety nor the ardor of their hearts has been able to create a higher ideal of man and of virtue than the ideal given by Christ of old. When it has been attempted, the result has been only grotesque.

—*Feodor Dostoevski*

If matter mute and inanimate, though changed by the forces of nature into a multitude of forms, can never die, will the spirit of man suffer annihilation when it has paid a brief visit, like a royal guest, to this tenement of clay?

—*William Jennings Bryan*

He said unto them, Have ye received the Holy Ghost since ye believed? And they said unto him, We have not so much as heard whether there be any Holy Ghost.

—*Acts 19:2*

My soul still flies above me for the quarry it shall find.

—*William Rose Benét*

Luke

1 And it came to pass, that, as he was praying in a certain place, when he ceased, one of his disciples said unto him, Lord, teach us to pray, as John also taught his disciples.

2 And he said unto them, When ye pray, say, Our Father which art in heaven, Hallowed be thy name. Thy kingdom come. Thy will be done, as in heaven, so in earth.

3 Give us day by day our daily bread.

4 And forgive us our sins; for we also forgive every one, that is indebted to us. And lead us not into temptation; but deliver us from evil.

5 And he said unto them, Which of you shall have a friend, and shall go unto him at midnight, and say unto him, Friend, lend me three loaves;

6 For a friend of mine in his journey is come to me, and I have nothing to set before him?

7 And he from within shall answer and say, Trouble me not: the door is now shut, and my children are with me in bed; I cannot rise and give thee.

8 I say unto you, Though he will not rise and give him, because he is his friend, yet because of his importunity he will rise and give him as many as he needeth.

9 And I say unto you, Ask, and it shall be given you; seek, and ye shall find; knock, and it shall be opened unto you.

10 For every one that asketh receiveth; and he that seeketh findeth; and to him that knocketh it shall be opened.

11 If a son shall ask bread of any of you that is a father, will he give him a stone? or if he ask a fish, will he for a fish give him a serpent?

12 Or if he shall ask an egg, will he offer him a scorpion?

13 If ye then, being evil, know how to give good gifts unto your children: how much more shall your heavenly Father give the Holy Spirit to them that ask him?

14 And he was casting out a devil, and it was dumb. And it came to pass, when the devil was gone out, the dumb spake; and the people wondered.

15 But some of them said, He casteth out devils through Beelzebub the chief of the devils.

17 But he, knowing their thoughts, said unto them, Every kingdom divided against itself is brought to desolation; and a house divided against a house falleth.

18 If Satan also be divided against himself, how shall his kingdom stand? because ye say that I cast out devils through Beelzebub.

19 And if I by Beelzebub cast out devils, by whom do your sons cast them out? therefore shall they be your judges.

20 But if I with the finger of God cast out devils, no doubt the kingdom of God is come upon you.

23 He that is not with me is against me: and he that gathereth not with me scattereth.

Ask and you will receive—even the Holy Spirit.

If this country had more respect for divine guidance it might have less need for guided missiles.

—Chilton

You cannot trace the guidance of the Spirit of God, or diagnose His operations in the secret rooms of the soul. He seems at times to let good go, and to bring instead good out of evil, and light into voluntary darkness.

—R. H. Benson

Be not forgetful of prayer. Every time you pray, if your prayer is sincere, there will be new feeling and new meaning in it, which will give you fresh courage, and you will understand that prayer is an education.

—Feodor Dostoevski

Do you ask where the Supreme God dwells? In the soul. And unless the soul be pure and holy, there is no room in it for God.

—Seneca

All His glory and beauty come from within, and there He delights to dwell. His visits there are frequent, His conversations sweet, His comforts refreshing, and His peace passing all understanding.

—Thomas à Kempis

Behold my servant, whom I uphold; mine elect, in whom my soul delighteth; I have put my spirit upon him.

—Isaiah 42:1

John

15 If ye love me, keep my commandments.

16 And I will pray the Father, and he shall give you another Comforter, that he may abide with you for ever;

17 *Even* the Spirit of truth; whom the world cannot receive, because it seeth him not, neither knoweth him: but ye know him; for he dwelleth with you, and shall be in you.

18 I will not leave you comfortless: I will come to you.

19 Yet a little while, and the world seeth me no more; but ye see me: because I live, ye shall live also.

20 At that day ye shall know that I *am* in my Father, and ye in me, and I in you.

21 He that hath my commandments, and keepeth them, he it is that loveth me: and he that loveth me shall be loved of my Father, and I will love him, and will manifest myself to him.

22 Judas saith unto him, not Iscariot, Lord, how is it that thou wilt manifest thyself unto us, and not unto the world?

23 Jesus answered and said unto him, If a man love me, he will keep my words: and my Father will love him, and we will come unto him, and make our abode with him.

24 He that loveth me not keepeth not my sayings: and the word which ye hear is not mine, but the Father's which sent me.

25 These things have I spoken unto you, being *yet* present with you.

26 But the Comforter, *which is* the Holy Ghost, whom the Father will send in my name, he shall teach you all things, and bring all things to your remembrance, whatsoever I have said unto you.

27 Peace I leave with you, my peace I give unto you: not as the world giveth, give I unto you. Let not your heart be troubled, neither let it be afraid.

CHAPTER 16

1 These things have I spoken unto you, that ye should not be offended.

2 They shall put you out of the synagogues: yea, the time cometh, that whosoever killeth you will think that he doeth God service.

3 And these things will they do unto you, because they have not known the Father, nor me.

4 But these things have I told you, that when the time shall come, ye may remember that I told you of them. And these things I said not unto you at the beginning, because I was with you.

5 But now I go my way to him that sent me; and none of you asketh me. Whither goest thou?

6 But because I have said these things unto you, sorrow hath filled your heart.

7 Nevertheless I tell you the truth; It is expedient for you that I go away: for if I go not away, the Comforter will not come unto you; but if I depart, I will send him unto you.

The Holy Spirit is willing to be our counselor and companion.

A gift is freely given, and expects no return. Its reason is love. What is first given is love; that is the first gift. The Holy Ghost comes forth as the substance of love, and *Gift* is His proper name.

—*Thomas Aquinas*

Humility is not denying the power you have but admitting that the power you have comes through you and not from you. To deny your power is to lie. We . . . simply have to admit that power comes through us and not from us.

—*Fred Smith*

The whole future of the human race depends on bringing the individual soul more completely and fully under sway of the Holy Spirit.

—*Isaac T. Hecker*

I should as soon attempt to raise flowers if there were no atmosphere, or produce fruits if there were neither light nor heat, as to regenerate men if I did not believe there was a Holy Spirit.

—*Henry Ward Beecher*

The Spirit also helpeth our infirmities: for we know not what we should pray for as we ought: but the Spirit itself maketh intercession for us with groanings which cannot be uttered. And he that searcheth the hearts knoweth what is the mind of the Spirit, because he maketh intercession for the saints according to the will of God.

—*Romans 8:26,27*

Arts

22 Ye men of Israel, hear these words; Jesus of Nazareth, a man approved of God among you by miracles and wonders and signs, which God did by him in the midst of you, as ye yourselves also know:

23 Him, being delivered by the determinate counsel and foreknowledge of God, ye have taken, and by wicked hands have crucified and slain:

24 Whom God hath raised up, having loosed the pains of death: because it was not possible that he should be holden of it.

25 For David speaketh concerning him, I foresaw the Lord always before my face; for he is on my right hand, that I should not be moved:

26 Therefore did my heart rejoice, and my tongue was glad; moreover also my flesh shall rest in hope:

27 Because thou wilt not leave my soul in hell, neither wilt thou suffer thine Holy One to see corruption.

28 Thou hast made known to me the ways of life; thou shalt make me full of joy with thy countenance.

29 Men *and* brethren, let me freely speak unto you of the patriarch David, that he is both dead and buried, and his sepulchre is with us unto this day.

30 Therefore being a prophet, and knowing that God had sworn with an oath to him, that of the fruit of his loins, according to the flesh, he

would raise up Christ to sit on his throne;

31 He, seeing this before, spake of the resurrection of Christ, that his soul was not left in hell, neither his flesh did see corruption.

32 This Jesus hath God raised up, whereof we all are witnesses.

33 Therefore being by the right hand of God exalted, and having received of the Father the promise of the Holy Ghost, he hath shed forth this, which ye now see and hear.

34 For David is not ascended into the heavens: but he saith himself, The Lord said unto my Lord, Sit thou on my right hand,

35 Until I make thy foes thy footstool.

36 Therefore let all the house of Israel know assuredly, that God hath made that same Jesus, whom ye have crucified, both Lord and Christ.

37 Now when they heard *this,* they were pricked in their heart, and said unto Peter and to the rest of the apostles, Men *and* brethren, what shall we do?

38 Then Peter said unto them, Repent, and be baptized every one of you in the name of Jesus Christ for the remission of sins, and ye shall receive the gift of the Holy Ghost.

39 For the promise is unto you, and to your children, and to all that are afar off, *even* as many as the Lord our God shall call.

The power of the Holy Spirit is available to you.

The whole aim of the science of perfection in Christ is to instruct men how to remove the hindrances in the way of the action of the Holy Spirit, and how to cultivate those virtues which are most favorable to His solicitations and inspirations. Thus the sum of spiritual life consists in observing and yielding to the movements of the Spirit of God in our soul, employing for this purpose all the exercises of prayer, spiritual reading, the practice of virtues, and good works.

—Isaac T. Hecker

Spiritual natures are on the summits of creation; there is nothing but God above them.

—Archbishop Ullathorne

Whosoever speaketh against the Holy Ghost, it shall not be forgiven him, neither in this world, neither in the world to come.

—Matthew 12:32

The Holy Spirit is not an inferior nature to the Father and the Son, but, so to say, cosubstantial and coeternal.

—Augustine

It is a dangerous grieving of the spirit, when, instead of drawing ourselves to the Spirit, we will labor to draw the Spirit to us.

—Richard Sibbes

By a Carpenter mankind was created and made, and only by that Carpenter can mankind be repaired.

—Desiderius Erasmus

Arts

8 And Stephen, full of faith and power, did great wonders and miracles among the people.

9 Then there arose certain of the synagogue, which is called *the synagogue* of the Libertines, and Cyrenians, and Alexandrians, and of them of Cilicia and of Asia, disputing with Stephen.

10 And they were not able to resist the wisdom and the spirit by which he spake.

11 Then they suborned men, which said, We have heard him speak blasphemous words against Moses, and *against* God.

12 And they stirred up the people, and the elders, and the scribes, and came upon *him*, and caught him, and brought *him* to the council,

13 And set up false witnesses, which said, This man ceaseth not to speak blasphemous words against this holy place, and the law:

CHAPTER 7

1 Then said the high priest, Are these things so?

2 And he said, Men, brethren, and fathers, hearken; . . . .

48 Howbeit the Most High dwelleth not in temples made with hands; as saith the prophet,

49 Heaven *is* my throne, and earth *is* my footstool: what house will ye build me? saith the Lord: or what *is* the place of my rest?

50 Hath not my hand made all these things?

51 Ye stiffnecked and uncircumcised in heart and ears, ye do always resist the Holy Ghost: as your fathers *did,* so *do* ye.

52 Which of the prophets have not your fathers persecuted? and they have slain them which showed before of the coming of the Just One; of whom ye have been now the betrayers and murderers:

53 Who have received the law by the disposition of angels, and have not kept *it.*

54 When they heard these things, they were cut to the heart, and they gnashed on him with *their* teeth.

55 But he, being full of the Holy Ghost, looked up steadfastly into heaven, and saw the glory of God, and Jesus standing on the right hand of God,

56 And said, Behold, I see the heavens opened, and the Son of man standing on the right hand of God.

57 Then they cried out with a loud voice, and stopped their ears, and ran upon him with one accord,

58 And cast *him* out of the city, and stoned *him:* and the witnesses laid down their clothes at a young man's feet, whose name was Saul.

59 And they stoned Stephen, calling upon *God,* and saying, Lord Jesus, receive my spirit.

60 And he kneeled down, and cried with a loud voice, Lord, lay not this sin to their charge. And when he had said this, he fell asleep.

Do you resist the Holy Spirit?

It is amazing how much God can accomplish through an imperfect person who has put all his imperfections completely at God's disposal.

—Unknown

Whatever we are, we are that by divine goodness; and this goodness is specially attributed to the Holy Spirit.

—Pope Leo XIII

Our Creator would never have made such lovely days and have given us the deep hearts to enjoy them, above and beyond all thought, unless we were meant to be immortal.

—Nathaniel Hawthorne

The word "Comforter" as applied to the Holy Spirit needs to be translated by some vigorous term. Literally, it means "with strength." Jesus promised His followers that "The Strengthener" would be with them forever. This promise is no lullaby for the fainthearted. It is a blood transfusion for courageous living.

—E. Paul Hovey

The more a man is united within himself, and interiorly simple, the more and higher things doth he understand without labor; because he receiveth the light of understanding from above.

—Thomas à Kempis

It is difficult to make a man miserable while he feels he is worthy of himself and claims kindred to the great God who made him.

—Abraham Lincoln

Romans

1 *There is* therefore now no condemnation to them which are in Christ Jesus, who walk not after the flesh, but after the Spirit.

2 For the law of the Spirit of life in Christ Jesus hath made me free from the law of sin and death.

3 For what the law could not do, in that it was weak through the flesh, God sending his own Son in the likeness of sinful flesh, and for sin, condemned sin in the flesh:

4 That the righteousness of the law might be fulfilled in us, who walk not after the flesh, but after the Spirit.

5 For they that are after the flesh do mind the things of the flesh; but they that are after the Spirit, the things of the Spirit.

6 For to be carnally minded *is* death; but to be spiritually minded *is* life and peace.

7 Because the carnal mind *is* enmity against God: for it is not subject to the law of God, neither indeed can be.

8 So then they that are in the flesh cannot please God.

9 But ye are not in the flesh, but in the Spirit, if so be that the Spirit of God dwell in you. Now if any man have not the Spirit of Christ, he is none of his.

10 And if Christ *be* in you, the body *is* dead because of sin; but the Spirit *is* life because of righteousness.

11 But if the Spirit of him that raised up Jesus from the dead dwell in you, he that raised up Christ from the dead shall also quicken your mortal bodies by his Spirit that dwelleth in you.

12 Therefore, brethren, we are debtors, not to the flesh, to live after the flesh.

13 For if ye live after the flesh, ye shall die: but if ye through the Spirit do mortify the deeds of the body, ye shall live.

14 For as many as are led by the Spirit of God, they are the sons of God.

15 For ye have not received the spirit of bondage again to fear; but ye have received the Spirit of adoption, whereby we cry, Abba, Father.

16 The Spirit itself beareth witness with our spirit, that we are the children of God:

17 And if children, then heirs; heirs of God, and joint heirs with Christ: if so be that we suffer with *him,* that we may be also glorified together.

18 For I reckon that the sufferings of this present time *are* not worthy *to be compared* with the glory which shall be revealed in us.

24 For we are saved by hope: but hope that is seen is not hope: for what a man seeth, why doth he yet hope for?

25 But if we hope for that we see not, *then* do we with patience wait for *it.*

Are you led by the Spirit of God?

We can easily forgive a child who is afraid of the dark; the real tragedy of life is when men are afraid of the light.

—Plato

No inferior form of energy can be simply converted into a superior form unless at the same time a source of higher value lends it support.

—Carl Jung

When it comes to the control of our lives, we are either "body" men or "spirit" men.

—Eric Lindholm

There is something in man which your science cannot satisfy.

—Thomas Carlyle

The soul has this proof of its divinity: that divine things delight it.

—Seneca

Fear God and where you go men will think they walk in hallowed cathedrals.

—Ralph Waldo Emerson

When men surrender themselves to the Spirit of God, they will learn more concerning God and Christ and the Atonement and immortality in a week, than they would learn in a lifetime, apart from the Spirit.

—John Brown

1 Corinthians

1 And I, brethren, when I came to you, came not with excellency of speech or of wisdom, declaring unto you the testimony of God.

2 For I determined not to know any thing among you, save Jesus Christ, and him crucified.

3 And I was with you in weakness, and in fear, and in much trembling.

4 And my speech and my preaching *was* not with enticing words of man's wisdom, but in demonstration of the Spirit and of power:

5 That your faith should not stand in the wisdom of men, but in the power of God.

6 Howbeit we speak wisdom among them that are perfect: yet not the wisdom of this world, nor of the princes of this world, that come to nought:

7 But we speak the wisdom of God in a mystery, *ever* the hidden *wisdom,* which God ordained before the world unto our glory;

8 Which none of the princes of this world knew: for had they known *it,* they would not have crucified the Lord of glory.

9 But as it is written, Eye hath not seen, nor ear heard, neither have entered into the heart of man, the things which God hath prepared for them that love him.

10 But God hath revealed *them* unto us by his Spirit: for the Spirit searcheth all things, yea, the deep things of God.

11 For what man knoweth the things of a man, save the spirit of man which is in him? even so the things of God knoweth no man, but the Spirit of God.

12 Now we have received, not the spirit of the world, but the Spirit which is of God; that we might know the things that are freely given to us of God.

13 Which things also we speak, not in the words which man's wisdom teacheth, but which the Holy Ghost teacheth; comparing spiritual things with spiritual.

14 But the natural man receiveth not the things of the Spirit of God: for they are foolishness unto him: neither can he know *them,* because they are spiritually discerned.

15 But he that is spiritual judgeth all things, yet he himself is judged of no man.

16 For who hath known the mind of the Lord, that he may instruct him? But we have the mind of Christ.

The Holy Spirit alone equips one to comprehend the things of God.

The spiritual life . . . means the ever more perfect and willing association of the invisible human spirit with the invisible divine Spirit for all purposes.

—Evelyn Underhill

Notice carefully, O pilgrim, the law of thy progress: after thou hast buried and done to death the concupiscences, thou wilt come to the wide open spaces of beatitude.

—Origen

You cannot run away from a weakness; you must some time fight it out or perish; and if that be so, why not now, and where you stand?

—Robert Louis Stevenson

Only by the supernatural is man strong; nothing is so weak as an egotist.

—Ralph Waldo Emerson

Let each of us remember that he will make progress in all spiritual things only insofar as he rids himself of self-love, self-will, self-interest.

—Ignatius of Loyola

No man ever prayed heartily without learning something.

—Ralph Waldo Emerson

Galatians

16 *This* I say then, Walk in the Spirit, and ye shall not fulfil the lust of the flesh.

17 For the flesh lusteth against the Spirit, and the Spirit against the flesh: and these are contrary the one to the other; so that ye cannot do the things that ye would.

18 But if ye be led of the Spirit, ye are not under the law.

19 Now the works of the flesh are manifest, which are *these,* Adultery, fornication, uncleanness, lasciviousness,

20 Idolatry, witchcraft, hatred, variance, emulations, wrath, strife, seditions, heresies.

21 Envyings, murders, drunkenness, revelings, and such like: of the which I tell you before, as I have also told *you* in time past, that they which do such things shall not inherit the kingdom of God.

22 But the fruit of the Spirit is love, joy, peace, long-suffering, gentleness, goodness, faith,

23 Meekness, temperance: against such there is no law.

24 And they that are Christ's have crucified the flesh with the affections and lusts.

25 If we live in the Spirit, let us also walk in the Spirit.

26 Let us not be desirous of vain-glory, provoking one another, envying one another.

CHAPTER 6

1 Brethren, if a man be overtaken in a fault, ye which are spiritual, restore such an one in the spirit of meekness; considering thyself, lest thou also be tempted.

2 Bear ye one another's burdens, and so fulfil the law of Christ.

3 For if a man think himself to be something, when he is nothing, he deceiveth himself.

4 But let every man prove his own work, and then shall he have rejoicing in himself alone, and not in another.

5 For every man shall bear his own burden.

6 Let him that is taught in the word communicate unto him that teacheth in all good things.

7 Be not deceived; God is not mocked: for whatsoever a man soweth, that shall he also reap.

8 For he that soweth to his flesh shall of the flesh reap corruption; but he that soweth to the Spirit shall of the Spirit reap life everlasting.

9 And let us not be weary in well doing: for in due season we shall reap, if we faint not.

10 As we have therefore opportunity, let us do good unto all *men,* especially unto them who are of the household of faith.

The Holy Spirit is our only hope of becoming and staying good men.

The steady discipline of friendship with Jesus results in men becoming like Him.

—*Harry Emerson Fosdick*

It is not more strange that there should be evil spirits than evil men—evil unembodied spirits than evil embodied spirits.

—*Samuel Johnson*

Everything science has taught me—and continues to teach me—strengthens my belief in the continuity of our spiritual existence after death.

—*Werner von Braun*

It is the oldest temptation in the world, and the most fruitful parent of sins, and the most dangerous temptation—in that it contains so much truth—to regard self rather than God as the center in which spiritual effort must originate.

—*R. H. Benson*

Now what the soul is to the body of man, the Holy Spirit is in the body of Christ, which is the church. The Holy Spirit does that in the whole church, which the soul does in all the members of a single body.

—*Augustine*

The way of the spiritual path is strewn with the wrecks of souls that might have been friends of Christ.

—*R. H. Benson*

1 John

1 Beloved, believe not every spirit, but try the spirits whether they are of God: because many false prophets are gone out into the world.

2 Hereby know ye the Spirit of God: Every spirit that confesseth that Jesus Christ is come in the flesh is of God:

3 And every spirit that confesseth not that Jesus Christ is come in the flesh is not of God: and this is that *spirit* of antichrist, whereof ye have heard that it should come; and even now already is it in the world.

4 Ye are of God, little children, and have overcome them: because greater is he that is in you, than he that is in the world.

5 They are of the world: therefore speak they of the world, and the world heareth them.

6 We are of God: he that knoweth God heareth us; he that is not of God heareth not us. Hereby know we the spirit of truth, and the spirit of error.

7 Beloved, let us love one another: for love is of God; and every one that loveth is born of God, and knoweth God.

8 He that loveth not knoweth not God; for God is love.

9 In this was manifested the love of God toward us, because that God sent his only begotten Son into the world, that we might live through him.

10 Herein is love, not that we loved God, but that he loved us, and sent his Son *to be* the propitiation for our sins.

11 Beloved, if God so loved us, we ought also to love one another.

12 No man hath seen God at any time. If we love one another, God dwelleth in us, and his love is perfected in us.

13 Hereby know we that we dwell in him, and he in us, because he hath given us of his Spirit.

14 And we have seen and do testify that the Father sent the Son *to be* the Saviour of the world.

15 Whosoever shall confess that Jesus is the Son of God, God dwelleth in him, and he in God.

16 And we have known and believed the love that God hath to us. God is love; and he that dwelleth in love dwelleth in God, and God in him.

17 Herein is our love made perfect, that we may have boldness in the day of judgment: because as he is, so are we in this world.

18 There is no fear in love; but perfect love casteth out fear: because fear hath torment. He that feareth is not made perfect in love.

19 We love him, because he first loved us.

20 If a man say, I love God, and hateth his brother, he is a liar: for he that loveth not his brother whom he hath seen, how can he love God whom he hath not seen?

21 And this commandment have we from him, That he who loveth God love his brother also.

There is no mistaking the Spirit of God.

Reflections

The Cost Is
Everything —
The Reward,
"Abundant Life"

When I consider my crosses, tribulations, and temptations, I shame myself almost to death, thinking what are they in comparison to the suffering of my blessed Savior Jesus Christ.

—Martin Luther

After crosses and losses men grow humbler and wiser.

—Benjamin Franklin

Persecution often does in this life, what the last great day will do completely—separate the wheat from the tares.

—Milner

Know how sublime a thing it is,to suffer and be strong.

—Henry Wadsworth Longfellow

Christ is the key to the history of the world. Not only does all harmonize with the mission of Christ, but all is subordinate to it.

—Johannes von Muller

One with God is always a majority, but many a martyr has been burned at the stake while the votes were being counted.

—Thomas B. Reed

One person with a belief is equal to a force of ninety-nine who only have interests.

—John Stuart Mill

Matthew

16 Behold, I send you forth as sheep in the midst of wolves: be ye therefore wise as serpents, and harmless as doves.

17 But beware of men: for they will deliver you up to the councils, and they will scourge you in their synagogues;

18 And ye shall be brought before governors and kings for my sake, for a testimony against them and the Gentiles.

19 But when they deliver you up, take no thought how or what ye shall speak: for it shall be given you in that same hour what ye shall speak.

20 For it is not ye that speak, but the Spirit of your Father which speaketh in you.

22 And ye shall be hated of all *men* for my name's sake: but he that endureth to the end shall be saved.

24 The disciple is not above *his* master, nor the servant above his lord.

25 It is enough for the disciple that he be as his master, and the servant as his lord. If they have called the master of the house Beelzebub, how much more *shall they call* them of his household?

26 Fear them not therefore: for there is nothing covered, that shall not be revealed; and hid, that shall not be known.

27 What I tell you in darkness, *that* speak ye in light: and what ye hear in the ear, *that* preach ye upon the housetops.

28 And fear not them which kill the body, but are not able to kill the soul: but rather fear him which is able to destroy both soul and body in hell.

29 Are not two sparrows sold for a farthing? and one of them shall not fall on the ground without your Father.

30 But the very hairs of your head are all numbered.

31 Fear ye not therefore, ye are of more value than many sparrows.

32 Whosoever therefore shall confess me before men, him will I confess also before my Father which is in heaven.

33 But whosoever shall deny me before men, him will I also deny before my Father which is in heaven.

34 Think not that I am come to send peace on earth: I came not to send peace, but a sword.

35 For I am come to set a man at variance against his father, and the daughter against her mother, and the daughter-in-law against her mother-in-law.

36 And a man's foes *shall be* they of his own household.

37 He that loveth father or mother more than me is not worthy of me: and he that loveth son or daughter more than me is not worthy of me.

38 And he that taketh not his cross, and followeth after me, is not worthy of me.

39 He that findeth his life shall lose it: and he that loseth his life for my sake shall find it.

***Following Christ must take precedence
over all other relationships.***

Buying, possessing, accumulating, this is not worldliness. But doing this in the love of it, with no love to God paramount—doing it so that thoughts of God and eternity are an intrusion—doing it so that one's spirit is secularized in doing it—this is worldliness.

—Herrick Johnson

There is a terrible fact that if I hadn't heard the call of Christ, I might have been a physician in Harley Street being driven about in my Rolls-Royce.

—Sir Wilfred Grenfell

I count him braver who overcomes his desires than him who overcomes his enemies; for the hardest victory is victory over self.

—Aristotle

I believe the promises of God enough to venture an eternity on them.

—Isaac Watts

Fires cannot be made with dead embers, nor can enthusiasm be stirred by spiritless men.

—Baldwin

I hate to see things done by halves. If it be right, do it boldly; if it be wrong, leave it undone.

—Gilpin

There are important cases in which the difference between half a heart and a whole heart makes just the difference between signal defeat and a splendid victory.

—Andrew K. Boyd

Mark

13 And they brought young children to him, that he should touch them; and *his* disciples rebuked those that brought *them.*

14 But when Jesus saw it, he was much displeased, and said unto them, Suffer the little children to come unto me, and forbid them not; for of such is the kingdom of God.

15 Verily I say unto you, Whosoever shall not receive the kingdom of God as a little child, he shall not enter therein.

16 And he took them up in his arms, put *his* hands upon them, and blessed them.

17 And when he was gone forth into the way, there came one running, and kneeled to him, and asked him, Good Master, what shall I do that I may inherit eternal life?

18 And Jesus said unto him, Why callest thou me good? *there is* none good but one, *that is,* God.

19 Thou knowest the commandments, Do not commit adultery, Do not kill, Do not steal, Do not bear false witness, Defraud not, Honor thy father and mother.

20 And he answered and said unto him, Master, all these have I observed from my youth.

21 Then Jesus beholding him loved him, and said unto him, One thing thou lackest: go thy way, sell whatsoever thou hast, and give to the poor, and thou shalt have treasure in heaven: and come, take up the cross, and follow me.

22 And he was sad at that saying, and went away grieved: for he had great possessions.

23 And Jesus looked round about, and saith unto his disciples, How hardly shall they that have riches enter into the kingdom of God!

24 And the disciples were astonished at his words. But Jesus answereth again, and saith unto them, Children, how hard is it for them that trust in riches to enter into the kingdom of God!

25 It is easier for a camel to go through the eye of a needle, than for a rich man to enter into the kingdom of God.

26 And they were astonished out of measure, saying among themselves, Who then can be saved?

27 And Jesus looking upon them saith, With men *it is* impossible, but not with God: for with God all things are possible.

28 Then Peter began to say unto him, Lo, we have left all, and have followed thee.

29 And Jesus answered and said, Verily I say unto you, There is no man that hath left house, or brethren, or sisters, or father, or mother, or wife, or children, or lands, for my sake, and the gospel's,

30 But he shall receive a hundredfold now in this time, houses, and brethren, and sisters, and mothers, and children, and lands, with persecutions; and in the world to come eternal life.

31 But many *that are* first shall be last; and the last first.

What comes between you and Jesus Christ?

I think it is that nations are no better than the men who make them up, that national policy can arise no higher than the standards of the people, that every man's greatest contribution to national life is his own faith and integrity.

—Sam Shoemaker

When Christ calls a man, He bids him come and die. There are different kinds of dying, it is true; but the essence of discipleship is contained in these words.

—Dietrich Bonhoeffer

If I had three hundred men who feared nothing but God, hated nothing but sin, and were determined to know nothing among men but Jesus Christ and Him crucified, I would set the world on fire.

—John Wesley

The truest end of life is to know the Life that never ends.

—William Penn

One is happy in the world only when one forgets the world.

—Anatole France

The greatest proof of the Christ-like life for others, is not how far a man can logically analyze his reasons for believing, but how far in practice he will stake his life on his beliefs.

—T. S. Elliot

Luke

1 In the mean time, when there were gathered together an innumerable multitude of people, insomuch that they trode one upon another, he began to say unto his disciples first of all. Beware ye of the leaven of the Pharisees, which is hypocrisy.

2 For there is nothing covered, that shall not be revealed; neither hid, that shall not be known.

3 Therefore, whatsoever ye have spoken in darkness shall be heard in the light; and that which ye have spoken in the ear in closets shall be proclaimed upon the housetops.

4 And I say unto you my friends, Be not afraid of them that kill the body, and after that have no more that they can do.

5 But I will forewarn you whom ye shall fear: Fear him, which after he hath killed hath power to cast into hell; yea, I say unto you, Fear him.

8 Also I say unto you, Whosoever shall confess me before men, him shall the Son of man also confess before the angels of God:

9 But he that denieth me before men shall be denied before the angels of God.

10 And whosoever shall speak a word against the Son of man, it shall be forgiven him: but unto him that blasphemeth against the Holy Ghost it shall not be forgiven.

15 And he said unto them, Take heed, and beware of covetousness: for a man's life consisteth not in the abundance of the things which he possesseth.

16 And he spake a parable unto them, saying, The ground of a certain rich man brought forth plentifully:

17 And he thought within himself, saying, What shall I do, because I have no room where to bestow my fruits?

18 And he said, This will I do: I will pull down my barns, and build greater; and there will I bestow all my fruits and my goods.

19 And I will say to my soul, Soul, thou hast much goods laid up for many years; take thine ease, eat, drink, *and* be merry.

20 But God said unto him, *Thou* fool, this night thy soul shall be required of thee: then whose shall those things be, which thou hast provided?

21 So *is* he that layeth up treasure for himself, and is not rich toward God.

31 But rather seek ye the kingdom of God; and all these things shall be added unto you.

32 Fear not, little flock; for it is your Father's good pleasure to give you the kingdom.

33 Sell that ye have, and give alms; provide yourselves bags which wax not old, a treasure in the heavens that faileth not, where no thief approacheth, neither moth corrupteth.

34 For where your treasure is, there will your heart be also.

If we believe Jesus Christ is who He claims to be, then He deserves our total commitment.

He who knows no hardships will know no hardihood. He who faces no calamity will need no courage. Mysterious though it is, the characteristics in human nature which we love best grow in a soil with a strong mixture of troubles.

—Harry Emerson Fosdick

The martyr cannot be dishonored. Every lash inflicted is a tongue of flame; every prison a more illustrious abode; every burned book or house enlightens the world; every suppressed or expunged word reverberates through the earth from side to side. Hours of sanity and consideration are always arriving to communities, as to individuals, when truth is seen and the martyrs are justified.

—Ralph Waldo Emerson

It is defeat that turns bone to flint, and gristle to muscle, and makes men invincible, and forms those heroic natures that are now in ascendancy in the world. Do not then be afraid of defeat. You are never so near to victory as when defeated in a good cause.

—Henry Ward Beecher

If Christ comes to rule in the hearts of men, it will be because we take Him with us on the tractor, behind the desk, when we're making a sale to a customer, or when we're driving on the road.

—Alexander Nunn

When Christ came into my life, I came about like a well-handed ship.

—Robert Louis Stevenson

Philippians

8 For God is my record, how greatly I long after you all in the bowels of Jesus Christ.

9 And this I pray, that your love may abound yet more and more in knowledge and *in* all judgment;

10 That ye may approve things that are excellent; that ye may be sincere and without offence till the day of Christ;

11 Being filled with the fruits of righteousness, which are by Jesus Christ, unto the glory and praise of God.

12 But I would ye should understand, brethren, that the things *which happened* unto me have fallen out rather unto the furtherance of the Gospel;

13 So that my bonds in Christ are manifest in all the palace, and in all other *places;*

14 And many of the brethren in the Lord, waxing confident by my bonds, are much more bold to speak the word without fear.

15 Some indeed preach Christ even of envy and strife; and some also of good will:

18 What then? notwithstanding, every way, whether in pretence, or in truth, Christ is preached; and I therein do rejoice, yea, and will rejoice.

19 For I know that this shall turn to my salvation through your prayer, and the supply of the Spirit of Jesus Christ,

20 According to my earnest expectation and *my* hope, that in nothing I shall be ashamed, but *that* with all boldness, as always, *so* now also Christ shall be magnified in my body, whether *it be* by life, or by death.

21 For to me to live *is* Christ, and to die *is* gain.

22 But if I live in the flesh, this *is* the fruit of my labour: yet what I shall choose I wot not.

23 For I am in a strait betwixt two, having a desire to depart, and to be with Christ; which is far better:

24 Nevertheless to abide in the flesh *is* more needful for you.

25 And having this confidence, I know that I shall abide and continue with you all for your furtherance and joy of faith;

26 That your rejoicing may be more abundant in Jesus Christ for me by my coming to you again.

27 Only let your conversation be as it becometh the gospel of Christ: that whether I come and see you, or else be absent, I may hear of your affairs, that ye stand fast in one spirit, with one mind striving together for the faith of the gospel;

28 And in nothing terrified by your adversaries: which is to them an evident token of perdition, but to you of salvation, and that of God.

29 For unto you it is given in the behalf of Christ, not only to believe on him, but also to suffer for his sake;

30 Having the same conflict which ye saw in me, and now hear *to be* in me.

Live your life so that it honors Jesus Christ.

We need people today who will come out boldly for the values for which Christ died, which they will not barter for gold no matter who snubs or who sneers or who screams.

—*Joseph R. Sizoo*

Not only have vast numbers of Americans lost all sense of the sacred, the moral, and the ethical, but the spiritual leaders from both the laity and the priesthood are often found in the forefront of this irreligious pursuit of comfort rather than conviction—of accommodation rather than truth—of the pleasant life rather than the meaningful life.

—*Frank Carlson*

It is a wicked thing to be neutral between right and wrong.

—*Theodore Roosevelt*

It is curious—curious that physical courage should be so common in the world and moral courage so rare.

—*Mark Twain*

The argument for the risen Christ is the living followers of Christ.

—*Winifred Kirkland*

Money is not required to buy one necessity of the soul.

—*Henry David Thoreau*

How many toil to lay up riches which they never enjoy.

—*William Jay*

1 Thessalonians

1 But of the times and the seasons, brethren, ye have no need that I write unto you.

2 For yourselves know perfectly that the day of the Lord so cometh as a thief in the night.

3 For when they shall say, Peace and safety; then sudden destruction cometh upon them, as travail upon a woman with child; and they shall not escape.

4 But ye, brethren, are not in darkness, that that day should overtake you as a thief.

5 Ye are all the children of light, and the children of the day: we are not of the night, nor of darkness.

6 Therefore let us not sleep, as *do* others; but let us watch and be sober.

7 For they that sleep sleep in the night; and they that be drunken are drunken in the night.

8 But let us, who are of the day, be sober, putting on the breastplate of faith and love; and for a helmet, the hope of salvation.

9 For God hath not appointed us to wrath, but to obtain salvation by our Lord Jesus Christ,

10 Who died for us, that, whether we wake or sleep, we should live together with him.

11 Wherefore comfort yourselves together, and edify one another, even as also ye do.

12 And we beseech you, brethren, to know them which labor among you, and are over you in the Lord, and admonish you;

13 And to esteem them very highly in love for their work's sake. *And* be at peace among yourselves.

14 Now we exhort you, brethren, warn them that are unruly, comfort the feebleminded, support the weak, be patient toward all *men.*

15 See that none render evil for evil unto any *man;* but ever follow that which is good, both among yourselves, and to all *men.*

16 Rejoice evermore.

17 Pray without ceasing.

18 In every thing give thanks: for this is the will of God in Christ Jesus concerning you.

19 Quench not the Spirit.

20 Despise not prophesyings.

21 Prove all things; hold fast that which is good.

22 Abstain from all appearance of evil.

23 And the very God of peace sanctify you wholly; and *I pray God* your whole spirit and soul and body be preserved blameless unto the coming of our Lord Jesus Christ.

24 Faithful *is* he that calleth you, who also will do *it.*

25 Brethren, pray for us.

26 Greet all the brethren with a holy kiss.

27 I charge you by the Lord, that this epistle be read unto all the holy brethren.

28 The grace of our Lord Jesus Christ *be* with you. Amen.

What results are your best efforts bringing forth?

When the soul resolves to perform every duty, immediately it is conscious of the presence of God.

—Francis Bacon

. . . all too easily we confuse a fear of standing up for our own beliefs, a tendency to be more influenced by the convictions of others than by our own, or simply a lack of conviction—with the need that the strong and mature feel to give full weight to the arguments of the other side.

—Dag Hammarskjold

We were not put here on earth to play around. "Life is real: Life is earnest," Longfellow wrote. We are not here to "have fun," which seems to be the chief ambition of so many. There is work to be done. There are responsibilities to be met. Humanity needs the abilities of every man and woman.

—Alden Palmer

An era in human history is the life of Jesus, and its immense influence for good leaves all the perversion and superstition that has accrued almost harmless.

—Ralph Waldo Emerson

There are thousands hacking at the branches of evil to One who is striking at the root.

—Henry David Thoreau

Rest satisfied with doing well and leave others to talk of you as they please.

—Pythagoras

1 Timothy

3 If any man teach otherwise, and consent not to wholesome words, *even* the words of our Lord Jesus Christ, and to the doctrine which is according to godliness;

4 He is proud, knowing nothing, but doting about questions and strifes of words, whereof cometh envy, strife, railings, evil surmisings,

5 Perverse disputings of men of corrupt minds, and destitute of the truth, supposing that gain is godliness: from such withdraw thyself.

6 But godliness with contentment is great gain.

7 For we brought nothing into *this* world, *and it is* certain we can carry nothing out.

8 And having food and raiment, let us be therewith content.

9 But they that will be rich fall into temptation and a snare, and *into* many foolish and hurtful lusts, which drown men in destruction and perdition.

10 For the love of money is the root of all evil: which while some coveted after, they have erred from the faith, and pierced themselves through with many sorrows.

11 But thou, O man of God, flee these things; and follow after righteousness, godliness, faith, love, patience, meekness.

12 Fight the good fight of faith, lay hold on eternal life, whereunto thou art also called, and hast professed a good profession before many witnesses.

13 I give thee charge in the sight of God, who quickeneth all things, and *before* Christ Jesus, who before Pontius Pilate witnessed a good confession;

14 That thou keep *this* commandment without spot, unrebukable, until the appearing of our Lord Jesus Christ:

15 Which in his times he shall show, *who is* the blessed and only Potentate, the King of kings, and Lord of lords;

16 Who only hath immortality, dwelling in the light which no man can approach unto; whom no man hath seen, nor can see: to whom *be* honor and power everlasting. Amen.

17 Charge them that are rich in this world, that they be not highminded, nor trust in uncertain riches, but in the living God, who giveth us richly all things to enjoy;

18 That they do good, that they be rich in good works, ready to distribute, willing to communicate;

19 Laying up in store for themselves a good foundation against the time to come, that they may lay hold on eternal life.

20 O Timothy, keep that which is committed to thy trust, avoiding profane *and* vain babblings, and oppositions of science falsely so called:

21 Which some professing have erred concerning the faith. Grace *be* with thee. Amen.

Guard yourself—follow Jesus Christ.

Our confidence in Christ does not make us lazy, negligent or careless, but on the contrary it awakens us, urges us on, and makes us active in living righteous lives and doing good. There is no self-confidence to compare with this.

—Ulrich Zwingli

A life totally consecrated to God sees all of its tasks as God-appointed.

—Unknown

If you carefully fulfill the various duties of life, from a principle of obedience to your heavenly Father, you shall enjoy that peace which the world cannot give nor take away.

—Samuel Adams

God is searching for men who are unique, thoroughly saved, and filled to running over with His Spirit. God and the world need men who will stand in the gap. . . .

—Frank Carlson

God always has an angel of help for those who are willing to do their duty.

—T. C. Cuyler

When we can say "no" not only to things that are wrong and sinful, but also to things pleasant, profitable, and good which would hinder and clog our grand duties and our chief work, we shall understand more fully what life is worth and how to make the most of it.

—C. A. Stoddard

The serene, silent beauty of a holy life is the most powerful influence in the world, next to the might of God.

—Blaise Pascal

Titus

1 But speak thou the things which become sound doctrine:

2 That the aged men be sober, grave, temperate, sound in faith, in charity, in patience.

3 The aged women likewise, that *they be* in behavior as becometh holiness, not false accusers, not given to much wine, teachers of good things;

4 That they may teach the young women to be sober, to love their husbands, to love their children,

5 *To be* discreet, chaste, keepers at home, good, obedient to their own husbands, that the word of God be not blasphemed.

6 Young men likewise exhort to be sober-minded.

7 In all things showing thyself a pattern of good works: in doctrine *showing* uncorruptness, gravity, sincerity,

8 Sound speech, that cannot be condemned; that he that is of the contrary part may be ashamed, having no evil thing to say of you.

9 *Exhort* servants to be obedient unto their own masters, *and* to please *them* well in all things; not answering again;

10 Not purloining, but showing all good fidelity; that they may adorn the doctrine of God our Saviour in all things.

11 For the grace of God that bringeth salvation hath appeared to all men,

12 Teaching us that, denying ungodliness and worldly lusts, we should live soberly, righteously, and godly, in this present world;

13 Looking for that blessed hope, and the glorious appearing of the great God and our Saviour Jesus Christ;

14 Who gave himself for us, that he might redeem us from all iniquity, and purify unto himself a peculiar people, zealous of good works.

15 These things speak, and exhort, and rebuke with all authority. Let no man despise thee.

Good conduct flows naturally from a man who loves God.

No man can serve two masters. He cannot worship the God of peace and at the same time invoke the God of war.

—Clifford P. Morehouse

The yoke of God will not fit a stiff neck.

—Unknown

If you're centered on yourself, you're a problem. If you're centered on God, you're a person.

—Oren Arnold

A man may be lifted out of the slums without God, but only God can lift the slums out of him.

—Unknown

O Lord, reform the world—beginning with me.

—Unknown

The true wealth of a nation lies not in its gold or silver, but in its learnings, wisdom, and in the uprightness of its sons.

—Kahlil Gibran

God nowhere tells us to give up things for the sake of giving them up. He tells us to give them up for the sake of the only thing worth having—life with Himself.

—Oswald Chambers

1 Peter

1 Wherefore laying aside all malice, and all guile, and hypocrisies, and envies, and all evil speakings,

2 As newborn babes, desire the sincere milk of the word, that ye may grow thereby:

3 If so be ye have tasted that the Lord is gracious.

4 To whom coming, *as unto* a living stone, disallowed indeed of men, but chosen of God, *and* precious,

5 Ye also, as lively stones, are built up a spiritual house, a holy priesthood, to offer up spiritual sacrifices, acceptable to God by Jesus Christ.

6 Wherefore also it is contained in the Scripture, Behold, I lay in Sion a chief corner stone, elect, precious: and he that believeth on him shall not be confounded.

7 Unto you therefore which believe *he is* precious: but unto them which be disobedient, the stone which the builders disallowed, the same is made the head of the corner,

8 And a stone of stumbling, and a rock of offence, *even to them* which stumble at the word, being disobedient: whereunto also they were appointed.

9 But ye *are* a chosen generation, a royal priesthood, a holy nation, a peculiar people; that ye should shew forth the praises of him who hath called you out of darkness into his marvellous light:

10 Which in time past *were* not a people, but *are* now the people of God: which had not obtained mercy, but now have obtained mercy.

11 Dearly beloved, I beseech *you* as strangers and pilgrims, abstain from fleshly lusts, which war against the soul;

12 Having your conversation honest among the Gentiles: that, whereas they speak against you as evil doers, they may by *your* good works, which they shall behold, glorify God in the day of visitation.

13 Submit yourselves to every ordinance of man for the Lord's sake: whether it be to the king, as supreme;

14 Or unto governors, as unto them that are sent by him for the punishment of evil doers, and for the praise of them that do well.

15 For so is the will of God, that with well doing ye may put to silence the ignorance of foolish men:

16 As free, and not using *your* liberty for a cloak of maliciousness, but as the servants of God.

17 Honour all *men*. Love the brotherhood. Fear God. Honour the king.

18 Servants, *be* subject to *your* masters with all fear; not only to the good and gentle, but also to the froward.

19 For this *is* thankworthy, if a man for conscience toward God endure grief, suffering wrongfully.

Submit to God and not to your lust.

Reflections

Talking
with God

You pray in your distress and in your need; would that you might pray also in the fullness of your joy in the days of abundance.

—*Kahlil Gibran*

What greater calamity can fall upon a nation than the loss of worship.

—*Thomas Carlyle*

I used to pray that God would do this or that. Now I pray that God will make His will known to me.

—*Mme. Chiang Kai-Shek*

The best remedy for those who are afraid, lonely, or unhappy is to go outside, somewhere where they can be quite alone with the heavens, nature, and God. . . . I know that then there will always be comfort for every sorrow, whatever the circumstances may be.

—*Anne Frank*

The principal cause of my leanness and unfruitfulness is owing to an unaccountable backwardness to pray. I can write or read or converse or hear with a ready heart; but prayer is more spiritual and inward than any of these, and the more spiritual any duty is the more my carnal heart is apt to start from it. Prayer and patience and faith are never disappointed. When I can find my heart in frame and liberty for prayer, everything else is comparatively easy.

—*Richard Newton*

For nothing reaches the heart but what is from the heart, or pierces the conscience but what comes from a living conscience.

—*William Penn*

Psalms

1 Give ear to my prayer, O God; and hide not thyself from my supplication.

2 Attend unto me, and hear me: I mourn in my complaint, and make a noise;

3 Because of the voice of the enemy, because of the oppression of the wicked: for they cast iniquity upon me, and in wrath they hate me.

4 My heart is sore pained within me: and the terrors of death are fallen upon me.

5 Fearfulness and trembling are come upon me, and horror hath overwhelmed me.

6 And I said, Oh that I had wings like a dove! *for then* would I fly away, and be at rest.

7 Lo, *then* would I wander far off, and remain in the wilderness. Selah.

9 Destroy, O Lord, *and* divide their tongues: for I have seen violence and strife in the city.

10 Day and night they go about it upon the walls thereof: mischief also and sorrow *are* in the midst of it.

12 For *it was* not an enemy *that* reproached me; then I could have borne *it:* neither *was* it he that hated me *that* did magnify *himself* against me; then I would have hid myself from him:

13 But *it was* thou, a man mine equal, my guide, and mine acquaintance.

14 We took sweet counsel together, *and* walked unto the house of God in company.

15 Let death seize upon them, *and* let them go down quick into hell: for wickedness *is* in their dwellings, *and* among them.

16 As for me, I will call upon God; and the LORD shall save me.

17 Evening, and morning, and at noon, will I pray, and cry aloud: and he shall hear my voice.

18 He hath delivered my soul in peace from the battle *that was* against me: for there were many with me.

19 God shall hear, and afflict them, even he that abideth of old. Selah. Because they have no changes, therefore they fear not God.

20 He hath put forth his hands against such as be at peace with him: he hath broken his covenant.

21 *The words* of his mouth were smoother than butter, but war *was* in his heart: his words were softer than oil, yet *were* they drawn swords.

22 Cast thy burden upon the LORD, and he shall sustain thee: he shall never suffer the righteous to be moved.

23 But thou, O God, shalt bring them down into the pit of destruction: bloody and deceitful men shall not live out half their days; but I will trust in thee.

God cares—talk out your problems with Him.

I fear John Knox's prayers more than any army of ten thousand.

—Mary, Queen of Scotland

More things are wrought by prayer than this world dreams of.

—Alfred Tennyson

None can believe how powerful prayer is, and what it is able to effect, but those who have learned it by experience.

—Martin Luther

But above all he excelled in prayer. The inwardness and weight of his spirit, the reverence and solemnity of his address and behavior, and the fewness and fullness of his words have often struck even strangers with admiration as they used to reach others with consolation. The most awful, living, reverent frame I ever felt or beheld, I must say, was his prayer. And truly it was a testimony. He knew and lived nearer to the Lord than other men, for they that know Him most will see most reason to approach Him with reverence and fear.

—William Penn of George Fox

If the anointing which we bear come not from the Lord of Hosts, we are deceivers, since only in prayer can we obtain it. Let us continue instant, constant, fervent in supplication. Let your fleece lie on the thrashing-floor of supplication till it is wet with the dew of heaven.

—Charles Spurgeon

God is His own best evidence.

—Unknown

Daniel

7 All the presidents of the kingdom, the governors, and the princes, the counsellors, and the captains, have consulted together to establish a royal statute, and to make a firm decree, that whosoever shall ask a petition of any God or man for thirty days, save of thee, O king, he shall be cast into the den of lions.

9 Wherefore king Darius signed the writing and the decree.

10 Now when Daniel knew that the writing was signed, he went into his house; and his windows being open in his chamber toward Jerusalem, he kneeled upon his knees three times a day, and prayed, and gave thanks before his God, as he did aforetime.

11 Then these men assembled, and found Daniel praying and making supplication before his God.

12 Then they came near, and spake before the king concerning the king's decree, Hast thou not signed a decree, that every man that shall ask *a petition* of any God or man within thirty days, save of thee, O king, shall be cast into the den of lions? The king answered and said, The thing *is* true, according to the law of the Medes and Persians, which altereth not.

13 Then answered they and said before the king, That Daniel, which *is* of the children of the captivity of Judah, regardeth not thee, O king, nor the decree that thou hast signed, but maketh his petition three times a day.

16 Then the king commanded, and they brought Daniel, and cast *him* into the den of lions. *Now* the king spake and said unto Daniel, Thy God whom thou servest continually, he will deliver thee.

18 Then the king went to his palace, and passed the night fasting: neither were instruments of music brought before him: and his sleep went from him.

20 And when he came to the den, he cried with a lamentable voice unto Daniel: *and* the king spake and said to Daniel, O Daniel, servant of the living God, is thy God, whom thou servest continually, able to deliver thee from the lions?

22 My God hath sent his angel, and hath shut the lions' mouths, that they have not hurt me: forasmuch as before him innocency was found in me; and also before thee, O king, have I done no hurt.

25 Then king Darius wrote unto all people, nations, and languages, that dwell in all the earth; Peace be multiplied unto you.

26 I make a decree, That in every dominion of my kingdom men tremble and fear before the God of Daniel: for he *is* the living God, and steadfast for ever, and his kingdom *that* which shall not be destroyed, and his dominion *shall be even* unto the end.

The God of Daniel is still alive and faithful to those who love Him.

How can you expect God to speak to you in that gentle and inward voice which melts the soul, when you are making so much noise with your rapid reflections? Be silent, and God will speak again.

—*Francois Fénelon*

The most pious prayer can become a blasphemy if he who offers it tolerates or helps to further conditions which are fatal to mankind, which render him unacceptable to God, or weaken his spiritual, moral, or religious sense.

—*Alfred Delp*

The fewer the words the better the prayer.

—*Martin Luther*

The most beautiful and most profound emotion we can experience is the sensation of the mystical. It is the power of all true science. . . . To know what is impenetrable to us really exists, manifesting itself as the highest wisdom and the most radiant beauty which our dull faculties can comprehend only in their most primitive forms—this knowledge, this feeling is at the center of true religiousness.

—*Albert Einstein*

The real tragedy of our prayers is not that God so often refuses to grant them. The tragedy is we so often ask for the wrong thing.

—*R. A. Knox*

Prayer—secret, fervent, believing prayer—lies at the root of all personal godliness.

—*Carey's Brotherhood*

Matthew

5 And when thou prayest, thou shalt not be as the hypocrites *are:* for they love to pray standing in the corners of the streets, that they may be seen of men. Verily I say unto you, They have their reward.

6 But thou, when thou prayest, enter into thy closet, and when thou hast shut the door, pray to thy Father which is in secret; and thy Father which seeth in secret shall reward thee openly.

7 But when ye pray, use not vain repetitions, as the heathen *do:* for they think that they shall be heard for their much speaking.

8 Be not ye therefore like unto them: for your Father knoweth what things ye have need of, before ye ask him.

9 After this manner therefore pray ye: Our Father which art in heaven, Hallowed be thy name.

10 Thy kingdom come. Thy will be done in earth, as *it is* in heaven.

11 Give us this day our daily bread.

12 And forgive us our debts, as we forgive our debtors.

13 And lead us not into temptation, but deliver us from evil: For thine is the kingdom, and the power, and the glory, for ever. Amen.

14 For if ye forgive men their trespasses, your heavenly Father will also forgive you:

15 But if ye forgive not men their trespasses, neither will your Father forgive your trespasses.

16 Moreover when ye fast, be not, as the hypocrites, of a sad countenance: for they disfigure their faces, that they may appear unto men to fast. Verily I say unto you, They have their reward.

17 But thou, when thou fastest, anoint thine head, and wash thy face;

18 That thou appear not unto men to fast, but unto thy Father which is in secret: and thy Father which seeth in secret shall reward thee openly.

19 Lay not up for yourselves treasures upon earth, where moth and rust doth corrupt, and where thieves break through and steal:

20 But lay up for yourselves treasures in heaven, where neither moth nor rust doth corrupt, and where thieves do not break through nor steal:

21 For where your treasure is, there will your heart be also.

22 The light of the body is the eye: if therefore thine eye be single, thy whole body shall be full of light.

23 But if thine eye be evil, thy whole body shall be full of darkness. If therefore the light that is in thee be darkness, how great *is* that darkness!

24 No man can serve two masters: for either he will hate the one, and love the other; or else he will hold to the one, and despise the other. Ye cannot serve God and mammon.

Prayer is a two-way conversation with God.

Prayer is a direct approach to the throbbing heart of the universe.

—*Israel Betton*

They never sought in vain that sought the Lord aright.

—*Robert Burns*

Lord, make me an instrument of your peace.
Where there is hatred, let me sow love;
Where there is injury, pardon;
Where there is doubt, faith;
Where there is despair, hope;
Where there is darkness, light;
Where there is sadness, joy.
Lord, grant that I may seek to comfort rather than to be comforted,
to understand rather than to be understood,
to love than to be loved.
For it is in giving that we receive,
By forgiving that we are forgiven,
and by dying that we awaken to eternal life.

—*Francis of Assisi*

The coldness of my love to Him who first loved me and has done so much for
me overwhelmed and confused me; and to complete my unworthy character, I had not only neglected to improve the grace given to the extent of my
duty and privilege, but for want of that improvement had, while abounding
in perplexing care and labor, declined from first zeal and love. I was
confounded, humbled myself, implored mercy, and renewed my covenant
to strive and devote myself unreservedly to the Lord.

—*John McKendree*

John

1 These words spake Jesus, and lifted up his eyes to heaven, and said, Father, the hour is come; glorify thy Son, that thy Son also may glorify thee:

2 As thou hast given him power over all flesh, that he should give eternal life to as many as thou hast given him.

3 And this is life eternal, that they might know thee the only true God, and Jesus Christ, whom thou hast sent.

4 I have glorified thee on the earth: I have finished the work which thou gavest me to do.

5 And now, O Father, glorify thou me with thine own self with the glory which I had with thee before the world was.

6 I have manifested thy name unto the men which thou gavest me out of the world: thine they were, and thou gavest them me; and they have kept thy word.

7 Now they have known that all things whatsoever thou hast given me are of thee.

8 For I have given unto them the words which thou gavest me; and they have received *them,* and have known surely that I came out from thee, and they have believed that thou didst send me.

9 I pray for them: I pray not for the world, but for them which thou hast given me; for they are thine.

10 And all mine are thine, and thine are mine; and I am glorified in them.

11 And now I am no more in the world, but these are in the world, and I come to thee. Holy Father, keep through thine own name those whom thou hast given me, that they may be one, as we *are.*

12 While I was with them in the world, I kept them in thy name: those that thou gavest me I have kept, and none of them is lost, but the son of perdition; that the Scripture might be fulfilled.

13 And now come I to thee; and these things I speak in the world, that they might have my joy fulfilled in themselves.

14 I have given them thy word; and the world hath hated them, because they are not of the world, even as I am not of the world.

15 I pray not that thou shouldest take them out of the world, but that thou shouldest keep them from the evil.

16 They are not of the world, even as I am not of the world.

17 Sanctify them through thy truth: thy word is truth.

18 As thou hast sent me into the world, even so have I also sent them into the world.

19 And for their sakes I sanctify myself, that they also might be sanctified through the truth.

What do you pray about?

The measure of the worth of our public activity for God is the private communion we have with Him.

—*Oswald Chambers*

There is but one question, and that is the will of God. That settles all other questions.

—*William E. Gladstone*

There are moments when, whatever attitude of the body, the soul is on its knees.

—*Victor Hugo*

I have never committed the least matter to God that I have not had reason for infinite praise.

—*Anna Shipton*

Faithful prayer always implies correlative exertion.

—*John Ruskin*

Silence is the element in which great things fashion themselves.

—*Thomas Carlyle*

For whatever high reasons, men of prayer must knock and knock—sometimes with bleeding knuckles in the dark.

—*George A. Buttrick*

Ephesians

1 For this cause I Paul, the prisoner of Jesus Christ for you Gentiles,

2 If ye have heard of the dispensation of the grace of God which is given me to you-ward:

3 How that by revelation he made known unto me the mystery; (as I wrote afore in few words;

4 Whereby, when ye read, ye may understand my knowledge in the mystery of Christ,)

5 Which in other ages was not made known unto the sons of men, as it is now revealed unto his holy apostles and prophets by the Spirit;

6 That the Gentiles should be fellow heirs, and of the same body, and partakers of his promise in Christ by the gospel:

7 Whereof I was made a minister, according to the gift of the grace of God given unto me by the effectual working of his power.

8 Unto me, who am less than the least of all saints, is this grace given, that I should preach among the Gentiles the unsearchable riches of Christ;

9 And to make all *men* see what *is* the fellowship of the mystery, which from the beginning of the world hath been hid in God, who created all things by Jesus Christ.

10 To the intent that now unto the principalities and powers in heavenly *places* might be known by the church the manifold wisdom of God,

11 According to the eternal purpose which he purposed in Christ Jesus our Lord:

12 In whom we have boldness and access with confidence by the faith of him.

13 Wherefore I desire that ye faint not at my tribulations for you, which is your glory.

14 For this cause I bow my knees unto the Father of our Lord Jesus Christ,

15 Of whom the whole family in heaven and earth is named,

16 That he would grant you, according to the riches of his glory, to be strengthened with might by his Spirit in the inner man;

17 That Christ may dwell in your hearts by faith; that ye, being rooted and grounded in love,

18 May be able to comprehend with all saints what *is* the breadth, and length, and depth, and height;

19 And to know the love of Christ, which passeth knowledge, that ye might be filled with all the fulness of God.

20 Now unto him that is able to do exceeding abundantly above all that we ask or think, according to the power that worketh in us,

21 Unto him *be* glory in the church by Christ Jesus throughout all ages, world without end. Amen.

Do you realize that others are praying for you?

He who prays without confidence cannot hope that his prayers will be granted.

—*Francois Fénelon*

When has any man of prayer told us that prayer has failed him?

—*George Bernanos*

I have found the greatest power in the world is the power of prayer.

—*Cecil B. DeMille*

Prayer is not a substitute for work; it is a desperate effort to work further and to be efficient beyond the range of one's powers.

—*Santayana*

If your knees are knocking, kneel on them.

—*Sign outside London Air Raid Post, W. W. II*

There cannot be a precise answer to a vague question.

—*Wendell Johnson*

Nothing in the affairs of men is worthy of great anxiety.

—*Plato*

Prayer is not overcoming God's reluctance; it is laying hold of His highest willingness.

—*Richard Chenevix Trench*

Philippians

1 Therefore, my brethren dearly beloved and longed for, my joy and crown, so stand fast in the Lord, *my* dearly beloved.

2 I beseech Euodias, and beseech Syntyche, that they be of the same mind in the Lord.

3 And I entreat thee also, true yokefellow, help those women which laboured with me in the gospel, with Clement also, and *with* other my fellow labourers, whose names *are* in the book of life.

4 Rejoice in the Lord always: *and* again I say, Rejoice.

5 Let your moderation be known unto all men. The Lord *is* at hand.

6 Be careful for nothing; but in every thing by prayer and supplication with thanksgiving let your requests be made known unto God.

7 And the peace of God, which passeth all understanding, shall keep your hearts and minds through Christ Jesus.

8 Finally, brethren, whatsoever things are true, whatsoever things *are* honest, whatsoever things *are* just, whatsoever things *are* pure, whatsoever things *are* lovely, whatsoever things *are* of good report; if *there be* any virtue, and if *there be* any praise, think on these things.

9 Those things, which ye have both learned, and received, and heard, and seen in me, do: and the God of peace shall be with you.

10 But I rejoiced in the Lord greatly, that now at the last your care of me hath flourished again; wherein ye were also careful, but ye lacked opportunity.

11 Not that I speak in respect of want: for I have learned, in whatsoever state I am, *therewith* to be content.

12 I know both how to be abased, and I know how to abound: every where and in all things I am instructed both to be full and to be hungry, both to abound and to suffer need.

13 I can do all things through Christ which strengtheneth me.

14 Notwithstanding, ye have well done, that ye did communicate with my affliction.

15 Now ye Philippians know also, that in the beginning of the gospel, when I departed from Macedonia, no church communicated with me as concerning giving and receiving, but ye only.

16 For even in Thessalonica ye sent once and again unto my necessity.

17 Not because I desire a gift: but I desire fruit that may abound to your account.

19 But my God shall supply all your need according to his riches in glory by Christ Jesus.

20 Now unto God and our Father *be* glory for ever and ever. Amen.

Be anxious for nothing—pray with confidence.

I have been driven many times to my knees by the overwhelming conviction that I had nowhere else to go. My own wisdom, and that of all about me, seemed insufficient for that day.

—Abraham Lincoln

There is no wisdom nor understanding nor counsel against the Lord.

—Proverbs 21:30

The intellect of the wise is like glass; it admits the light of heaven and reflects it.

—Julius Charles Hare

A little philosophy inclineth a man's mind to atheism, but depth in philosophy bringeth man's mind about to religion.

—Francis Bacon

What in me is dark
Illumine, and what is law raise and support
That to the height of that great argument
I may assert eternal Providence,
And justify the ways of God to men.

—John Milton

Wisdom is the right use of knowledge.

—Charles Spurgeon

True wisdom, that from above, is teachable, moving in toward the goal of completeness through that which it learns.

—E. D. Head

James

2 My brethren, count it all joy when ye fall into divers temptations;

3 Knowing *this*, that the trying of your faith worketh patience.

4 But let patience have *her* perfect work, that ye may be perfect and entire, wanting nothing.

5 If any of you lack wisdom, let him ask of God, that giveth to all *men* liberally, and upbraideth not; and it shall be given him.

6 But let him ask in faith, nothing wavering: for he that wavereth is like a wave of the sea driven with the wind and tossed.

7 For let not that man think that he shall receive any thing of the Lord.

8 A double minded man *is* unstable in all his ways.

12 Blessed *is* the man that endureth temptation: for when he is tried, he shall receive the crown of life, which the Lord hath promised to them that love him.

13 Let no man say when he is tempted, I am tempted of God: for God cannot be tempted with evil, neither tempteth he any man:

14 But every man is tempted, when he is drawn away of his own lust, and enticed.

15 Then when lust hath conceived, it bringeth forth sin; and sin, when it is finished, bringeth forth death.

16 Do not err, my beloved brethren.

17 Every good gift and every perfect gift is from above, and cometh down from the Father of lights, with whom is no variableness, neither shadow of turning.

19 Wherefore, my beloved brethren, let every man be swift to hear, slow to speak, slow to wrath:

20 For the wrath of man worketh not the righteousness of God.

21 Wherefore lay apart all filthiness and superfluity of naughtiness, and receive with meekness the engrafted word, which is able to save your souls.

22 But be ye doers of the word, and not hearers only, deceiving your own selves.

23 For if any be a hearer of the word, and not a doer, he is like unto a man beholding his natural face in a glass:

24 For he beholdeth himself, and goeth his way, and straightway forgetteth what manner of man he was.

25 But whoso looketh into the perfect law of liberty, and continueth *therein,* he being not a forgetful hearer, but a doer of the work, this man shall be blessed in his deed.

26 If any man among you seem to be religious, and bridleth not his tongue, but deceiveth his own heart, this man's religion *is* vain.

Ask God for wisdom.

Study universal holiness of life. Your whole usefulness depends on this. . . .
Give yourself to prayer, and get your texts, your thoughts, your words from
God. Luther spent his best three hours in prayer.

—Robert Murray McCheyne

Prayer is the first thing, the second thing, the third thing necessary. . . . Pray,
then, my dear brother; pray, pray, pray.

—Edward Payson

Dear Lord, who sought at dawn of day,
In solitary woods to pray,
In quietness we come to ask
Thy presence for our daily task.

—Harry Webb Farrington

If some people who follow Christ that have been complaining of their
ministers had said and acted less before men and had applied themselves
with all their might to cry to God for their ministers—had as it were, risen
and stormed heaven with their humble, fervent and incessant prayers for
them—they would have been much more in the way of success.

—Jonathan Edwards

I ought to pray before seeing any one. Often when I sleep long, or meet with
others early, it is eleven or twelve o'clock before I begin secret prayer. This is
a wretched system. It is unscriptural. Christ arose before day and went into a
solitary place. David says, "Early will I seek thee." I feel it is far better to begin
with God—to see His face first, to get my soul near Him before it is near
another.

—Robert Murray McCheyne

James

1 Go to now, *ye* rich men, weep and howl for your miseries that shall come upon *you.*

2 Your riches are corrupted, and your garments are motheaten.

3 Your gold and silver is cankered; and the rust of them shall be a witness against you, and shall eat your flesh as it were fire. Ye have heaped treasure together for the last days.

4 Behold, the hire of the labourers who have reaped down your fields, which is of you kept back by fraud, crieth: and the cries of them which have reaped are entered into the ears of the Lord of Sabaoth.

5 Ye have lived in pleasure on the earth, and been wanton; ye have nourished your hearts, as in a day of slaughter.

6 Ye have condemned *and* killed the just; *and* he doth not resist you.

7 Be patient therefore, brethren, unto the coming of the Lord. Behold, the husbandman waiteth for the precious fruit of the earth, and hath long patience for it, until he receive the early and latter rain.

8 Be ye also patient; stablish your hearts: for the coming of the Lord draweth nigh.

11 Behold, we count them happy which endure. Ye have heard of the patience of Job, and have seen the end of the Lord; that the Lord is very pitiful, and of tender mercy.

12 But above all things, my brethren, swear not, neither by heaven, neither by the earth, neither by any other oath: but let your yea be yea; and *your* nay, nay; lest ye fall into condemnation.

13 Is any among you afflicted? let him pray. Is any merry? let him sing psalms.

14 Is any sick among you? let him call for the elders of the church; and let them pray over him, anointing him with oil in the name of the Lord:

15 And the prayer of faith shall save the sick, and the Lord shall raise him up; and if he have committed sins, they shall be forgiven him.

16 Confess *your* faults one to another, and pray one for another, that he may be healed. The effectual fervent prayer of a righteous man availeth much.

17 Elias was a man subject to like passions as we are, and he prayed earnestly that it might not rain: and it rained not on the earth by the space of three years and six months.

18 And he prayed again, and the heaven gave rain, and the earth brought forth her fruit.

19 Brethren, if any of you do err from the truth, and one convert him;

20 Let him know, that he which converteth the sinner from the error of his way shall save a soul from death, and shall hide a multitude of sins.

The Lord loves to talk to you about everything.

Reflections

Search the
Scriptures

That Book, sir, is the rock on which this Republic rests.

—*Andrew Jackson*

The American nation from its first settlement in Jamestown to this hour is based upon and permeated by the Bible.

—*James Brewer*

My only hope for the world is in bringing the human mind into contact with divine revelation.

—*William E. Gladstone*

The Bible is no mere book, but a Living Creature, with a power that conquers all that oppose it.

—*Napoléon Bonaparte*

If we abide by the principles taught in the Bible, our country will go on prospering and to prosper; but if we and our posterity neglect its instructions and authority, no man can tell how sudden a catastrophe may overwhelm us and bury all our glory in profound obscurity.

—*Daniel Webster*

The Bible has always been regarded as part of the Common Law of England.

—*William Blackstone*

This is the Canon that will make Italy free."

—*Giuseppe Garibaldi*

The New Testament is the best Book the world has ever known or will ever know.

—*Charles Dickens*

Deuteronomy

1 Therefore thou shalt love the LORD thy God, and keep his charge, and his statutes, and his judgments, and his commandments, alway.

2 And know ye this day: for *I speak* not with your children which have not known, and which have not seen the chastisement of the LORD your God, his greatness, his mighty hand, and his stretched out arm,

7 But your eyes have seen all the great acts of the LORD which he did.

8 Therefore shall ye keep all the commandments which I command you this day, that ye may be strong, and go in and possess the land, whither ye go to possess it;

9 And that ye may prolong *your* days in the land, which the LORD sware unto your fathers to give unto them and to their seed, a land that floweth with milk and honey.

12 A land which the LORD thy God careth for: the eyes of the LORD thy God *are* always upon it, from the beginning of the year even unto the end of the year.

13 And it shall come to pass, if ye shall hearken diligently unto my commandments which I command you this day, to love the LORD your God, and to serve him with all your heart and with all your soul,

14 That I will give *you* the rain of your land in his due season, the first rain and the latter rain, that thou mayest gather in thy corn, and thy wine, and thine oil.

16 Take heed to yourselves, that your heart be not deceived, and ye turn aside, and serve other gods, and worship them;

17 And *then* the LORD's wrath be kindled against you, and he shut up the heaven, that there be no rain, and that the land yield not her fruit; and *lest* ye perish quickly from off the good land which the LORD giveth you.

18 Therefore shall ye lay up these my words in your heart and in your soul, and bind them for a sign upon your hand, that they may be as frontlets between yours eyes.

19 And ye shall teach them your children, speaking of them when thou sittest in thine house, and when thou walkest by the way, when thou liest down, and when thou risest up.

20 And thou shalt write them upon the doorposts of thine house, and upon thy gates:

21 That your days may be multiplied, and the days of your children, in the land which the LORD sware unto your fathers to give them, as the days of heaven upon the earth.

22 For if ye shall diligently keep all these commandments which I command you, to do them, to love the LORD your God, to walk in all his ways, and to cleave unto him;

Teach the Words of God to your children by deed and word.

I have known ninety-five of the world's great men in my time, and of them eighty-seven were followers of the Bible.

—*William E. Gladstone*

In all my perplexities and distresses, the Bible has never failed to give me light and strength.

—*Robert E. Lee*

I am profitably engaged reading the Bible. Take all of this Book upon reason that you can, and the balance on faith, and you will live and die a better man.

—*Abraham Lincoln*

Almost every man who has by his life-work added to the sum of human achievement of which the race is proud, almost every such man has based his work largely upon the teachings of the Bible.

—*Theodore Roosevelt*

I speak as a man of the world to men of the world, and I say to you: search the Scriptures. The Bible is the Book of all others to read at all ages and in all conditions of human life; not to be read once or twice or thrice through and then laid aside; but to be read in small portions of one or two chapters a day and never to be omitted by some overwhelming necessity.

—*John Quincy Adams*

There is no safer reliance than upon the God of our fathers, who has so singularly favored the American people in every national trial, and who will not forsake us so long as we obey His commandments and walk humbly in His footsteps.

—*William McKinley*

No lawyer can afford to be ignorant of the Bible.

—*Rufus Choate*

Psalms

1 Blessed *is* the man that walketh not in the counsel of the ungodly, nor standeth in the way of sinners, nor sitteth in the seat of the scornful.

2 But his delight *is* in the law of the LORD; and in his law doth he meditate day and night.

3 And he shall be like a tree planted by the rivers of water, that bringeth forth his fruit in his season; his leaf also shall not wither; and whatsoever he doeth shall prosper.

4 The ungodly *are* not so: but *are* like the chaff which the wind driveth away.

5 Therefore the ungodly shall not stand in the judgment, nor sinners in the congregation of the righteous.

6 For the LORD knoweth the way of the righteous: but the way of the ungodly shall perish.

CHAPTER 37

1 Fret not thyself because of evildoers, neither be thou envious against the workers of iniquity.

2 For they shall soon be cut down like the grass, and wither as the green herb.

3 Trust in the LORD, and do good; *so* shalt thou dwell in the land, and verily thou shalt be fed.

4 Delight thyself also in the LORD; and he shall give thee the desires of thine heart.

5 Commit thy way unto the LORD; trust also in him; and he shall bring *it* to pass.

6 And he shall bring forth thy righteousness as the light, and thy judgment as the noonday.

7 Rest in the LORD, and wait patiently for him: fret not thyself because of him who prospereth in his way, because of the man who bringeth wicked devices to pass.

8 Cease from anger, and forsake wrath: fret not thyself in any wise to do evil.

9 For evildoers shall be cut off: but those that wait upon the LORD, they shall inherit the earth.

10 For yet a little while, and the wicked *shall* not *be:* yea, thou shalt diligently consider his place, and it *shall* not *be.*

11 But the meek shall inherit the earth; and shall delight themselves in the abundance of peace.

12 The wicked plotteth against the just, and gnasheth upon him with his teeth.

13 The Lord shall laugh at him: for he seeth that his day is coming.

14 The wicked have drawn out the sword, and have bent their bow, to cast down the poor and needy, *and* to slay such as be of upright conversation.

15 Their sword shall enter into their own heart, and their bows shall be broken.

16 A little that a righteous man hath *is* better than the riches of many wicked.

Do you rely upon the counsel of men or of God?

The whole hope of human progress is suspended on the ever growing influence of the Bible.

—William Henry Seward

I always have said, and always will say, that the studious perusal of the sacred Volume will make better citizens, better fathers, and better husbands.

—Thomas Jefferson

Hold fast to the Bible as the sheet anchor of your liberties; write its precepts on your hearts and practice them in your lives. To the influence of this Book we are indebted for the progress made, and to this we must look as our guide in the future.

—Ulysses S. Grant

The Bible has been the Magna Charta of the poor and oppressed. The human race is not in a position to dispense with it.

—Thomas Huxley

The Bible is the greatest benefit which the human race has ever experienced.

—Immanuel Kant

All that I am I owe to Jesus Christ, revealed to me in His divine Book.

—David Livingstone

Give me a Bible and a candle and shut me up in a dungeon and I will tell you what the world is doing.

—Unknown

Is not my word like as a fire? saith the Lord; and like a hammer that breaketh the rock in pieces?

—Jeremiah 23:29

Psalms

DALETH

25 My soul cleaveth unto the dust: quicken thou me according to thy word.

26 I have declared my ways, and thou heardest me: teach me thy statutes.

27 Make me to understand the way of thy precepts: so shall I talk of thy wondrous works.

28 My soul melteth for heaviness: strengthen thou me according unto thy word.

29 Remove from me the way of lying: and grant me thy law graciously.

30 I have chosen the way of truth: thy judgments have I laid *before me.*

31 I have stuck unto thy testimonies: O LORD, put me not to shame.

32 I will run the way of thy commandments, when thou shalt enlarge my heart.

33 Teach me, O LORD, the way of thy statutes; and I shall keep it *unto* the end.

34 Give me understanding, and I shall keep thy law; yea, I shall observe it with *my* whole heart.

35 Make me to go in the path of thy commandments; for therein do I delight.

36 Incline my heart unto thy testimonies, and not to covetousness.

37 Turn away mine eyes from beholding vanity; *and* quicken thou me in thy way.

38 Stablish thy word unto thy servant, who *is devoted* to thy fear.

39 Turn away my reproach which I fear: for thy judgments *are* good.

40 Behold, I have longed after thy precepts: quicken me in thy righteousness.

VAU

41 Let thy mercies come also unto me, O LORD, *even* thy salvation, according to thy word.

42 So shall I have wherewith to answer him that reproacheth me: for I trust in thy word.

43 And take not the word of truth utterly out of my mouth; for I have hoped in thy judgments.

44 So shall I keep thy law continually for ever and ever.

45 And I will walk at liberty: for I seek thy precepts.

46 I will speak of thy testimonies also before kings, and will not be ashamed.

47 And I will delight myself in thy commandments, which I have loved.

48 My hands also will I lift up unto thy commandments, which I have loved; and I will meditate in thy statutes.

Are the commandments and laws of God exciting to you?

I thoroughly believe in a university education for both men and women; but . . . a knowledge of the Bible without a college education is more valuable than a college education without the Bible. Everyone who has a thorough knowledge of the Bible may truly be called educated, and no other learning . . . no matter how extensive . . . can form a proper substitute.

—William Lyon Phelps

Let mental culture go on advancing, let the natural sciences progress in ever greater extent and depth, and the human mind widen itself as much as it desires; beyond the elevation and moral culture of Christ's way as it shines forth in the Gospels, it will not go.

—Goethe

Let the men of science and learning expand their knowledge and probe with their researches every detail of the records which have been preserved to us from these dim ages. All they will do is to fortify the grand simplicity and essential accuracy of the recorded truths which have lighted so far the pilgrimage of man.

—Winston Churchill

For forty years I have loved the Word of God. I feel the blessed pages under my hand with special thankfulness as a rod and a staff to keep firm my steps through the valley of the shadow of depression and world calamity. Truly the Bible—the teaching of our Savior—is the only way out of the dark. If the wealth of things which we have in abundance has not knocked on our selfish hearts and opened them to the central message of Jesus, "Love ye one another," perhaps these days of widespread suffering will be the pointed instrument that will "stab [our] spirit broad awake."

—Helen Keller

But for this Book we could not know right from wrong.

—Abraham Lincoln

Psalms

MEM

97 O how love I thy law! it *is* my meditation all the day.

98 Thou through thy commandments hast made me wiser than mine enemies: for they *are* ever with me.

99 I have more understanding than all my teachers: for thy testimonies *are* my meditation.

100 I understand more than the ancients, because I keep thy precepts.

101 I have refrained my feet from every evil way, that I might keep thy word.

102 I have not departed from thy judgments: for thou hast taught me.

103 How sweet are thy words unto my taste! *yea, sweeter* than honey to my mouth.

104 Through thy precepts I get understanding: therefore I hate every false way.

NUN

105 Thy word *is* a lamp unto my feet, and a light unto my path.

106 I have sworn, and I will perform *it*, that I will keep thy righteous judgments.

107 I am afflicted very much: quicken me, O LORD, according unto thy word.

108 Accept, I beseech thee, the freewill offerings of my mouth, O LORD, and teach me thy judgments.

109 My soul *is* continually in my hand: yet do I not forget thy law.

110 The wicked have laid a snare for me: yet I erred not from thy precepts.

111 Thy testimonies have I taken as a heritage for ever: for they *are* the rejoicing of my heart.

112 I have inclined mine heart to perform thy statutes always, *even unto* the end.

SAMECH

113 I hate *vain* thoughts: but thy law do I love.

114 Thou *art* my hiding place and my shield: I hope in thy word.

115 Depart from me, ye evildoers: for I will keep the commandments of my God.

116 Uphold me according unto thy word, that I may live: and let me not be ashamed of my hope.

117 Hold thou me up, and I shall be safe: and I will have respect unto thy statutes continually.

118 Thou hast trodden down all them that err from thy statutes; for their deceit *is* falsehood.

119 Thou puttest away all the wicked of the earth *like* dross: therefore I love thy testimonies.

120 My flesh trembleth for fear of thee; and I am afraid of thy judgments.

Leave enough time in your schedule to search the Scriptures.

In this little Book will be found the solution to all the problems of the world.

—Calvin Coolidge

As a nation we are indebted to the Book of Books for our national ideals and representative institutions. Their preservation rests in adhering to its principles.

—Herbert Hoover

Take time to think and to pinpoint what's really important in your life.

—Alexander Reid Martin

All human discoveries seem to be made only for the purpose of confirming more and more the truths contained in the Holy Scriptures.

—John Herschel

So great is my veneration for the Bible that the earlier my children begin to read it, the more confident will be my hope that they will prove useful citizens to their country, and respectable members of society.

—John Quincy Adams

Sin will keep you from this Book. This Book will keep you from sin.

—Dwight L. Moody

The Bible is the one Book to which any thoughtful man may go with any honest question of life or destiny and find the answer of God by honest searching.

—John Ruskin

Mark

1 And he began again to teach by the sea side: and there was gathered unto him a great multitude, so that he entered into a ship, and sat in the sea; and the whole multitude was by the sea on the land.

2 And he taught them many things by parables, and said unto them in his doctrine,

3 Hearken; Behold, there went out a sower to sow:

4 And it came to pass, as he sowed, some fell by the wayside, and the fowls of the air came and devoured it up.

5 And some fell on stony ground, where it had not much earth; and immediately it sprang up, because it had no depth of earth:

6 But when the sun was up, it was scorched; and because it had no root, it withered away.

7 And some fell among thorns, and the thorns grew up, and choked it, and it yielded no fruit.

8 And other fell on good ground, and did yield fruit that sprang up and increased, and brought forth, some thirty, and some sixty, and some a hundred.

9 And he said unto them, He that hath ears to hear, let him hear.

10 And when he was alone, they that were about him with the twelve asked of him the parable.

11 And he said unto them, Unto you it is given to know the mystery of the kingdom of God: but unto them that are without, all *these* things are done in parables:

12 That seeing they may see, and not perceive; and hearing they may hear, and not understand; lest at any time they should be converted, and *their* sins should be forgiven them.

13 And he said unto them, Know ye not this parable? and how then will ye know all parables?

14 The sower soweth the word.

15 And these are they by the wayside, where the word is sown; but when they have heard, Satan cometh immediately, and taketh away the word that was sown in their hearts.

16 And these are they likewise which are sown on stony ground; who, when they have heard the word, immediately receive it with gladness;

17 And have no root in themselves, and so endure but for a time: afterward, when affliction or persecution ariseth for the word's sake, immediately they are offended.

18 And these are they which are sown among thorns; such as hear the word,

19 And the cares of this world, and the deceitfulness of riches, and the lusts of other things entering in, choke the word, and it becometh unfruitful.

20 And these are they which are sown on good ground; such as hear the word, and receive *it,* and bring forth fruit, some thirtyfold, some sixty, and some a hundred.

Remember these four ways to respond to the Word of God.

Men do not reject the Bible because it contradicts itself, but because it contradicts them.

—Unknown

The existence of the Bible, as a Book for the people, is the greatest benefit which the human race has ever experienced. Every attempt to belittle it is a crime against humanity.

—Immanuel Kant

It is impossible to enslave mentally or socially a Bible-reading people. The principles of the Bible are the groundwork of human freedom.

—Horace Greeley

It is proper to show my colors and avow my sentiments. I give them without figure of rhetoric or form of argument, and simply declare that I believe that there is a God—a personal, infinitely gracious Creator and Father of all; a God of goodness, justice, and holiness; the God of the Bible. I also declare my belief that the Bible is the Word of God, and that the central idea of His inspired revelation is Christ.

—Lucious Q. C. Lamar

If truth be not diffused, error will be; if God and His work are not known and received, the devil and his works will gain ascendency; if the evangelical Volume does not reach every hamlet, the pages of a corrupt and licentious literature will; if the power of the gospel is not felt through the length and breadth of the land, anarchy and misrule, degradation and misery, corruption and darkness, will reign without mitigation or end.

—Daniel Webster

This book of the law shall not depart out of thy mouth; but thou shalt meditate therein day and night, that thou mayest observe to do according to all that is written therein: for then thou shalt make thy way prosperous, and then thou shalt have good success.

—Joshua 1:8

II Timothy

1 This know also, that in the last days perilous times shall come.

2 For men shall be lovers of their own selves, covetous, boasters, proud, blasphemers, disobedient to parents, unthankful, unholy,

3 Without natural affection, trucebreakers, false accusers, incontinent, fierce, despisers of those that are good,

4 Traitors, heady, highminded, lovers of pleasures more than lovers of God;

5 Having a form of godliness, but denying the power thereof: from such turn away.

6 For of this sort are they which creep into houses, and lead captive silly women laden with sins, led away with divers lusts,

7 Ever learning, and never able to come to the knowledge of the truth.

8 Now as Jannes and Jambres withstood Moses, so do these also resist the truth: men of corrupt minds, reprobate concerning the faith.

9 But they shall proceed no further: for their folly shall be manifest unto all *men,* as their's also was.

10 But thou hast fully known my doctrine, manner of life, purpose, faith, longsuffering, charity, patience,

11 Persecutions, afflictions, which came unto me at Antioch, at Iconium, at Lystra; what persecutions I endured: but out of *them* all the Lord delivered me.

12 Yea, and all that will live godly in Christ Jesus shall suffer persecution.

13 But evil men and seducers shall wax worse and worse, deceiving, and being deceived.

14 But continue thou in the things which thou hast learned and hast been assured of, knowing of whom thou hast learned *them;*

15 And that from a child thou hast known the holy scriptures, which are able to make thee wise unto salvation through faith which is in Christ Jesus.

16 All scripture *is* given by inspiration of God, and *is* profitable for doctrine, for reproof, for correction, for instruction in righteousness:

17 That the man of God may be perfect, throughly furnished unto all good works.

CHAPTER 4

1 I charge *thee* therefore before God, and the Lord Jesus Christ, who shall judge the quick and the dead at his appearing and his kingdom;

2 Preach the word; be instant in season, out of season; reprove, rebuke, exhort with all longsuffering and doctrine.

3 For the time will come when they will not endure sound doctrine; but after their own lusts shall they heap to themselves teachers, having itching ears;

4 And they shall turn away *their* ears from the truth, and shall be turned unto fables.

Teach the Bible to your children—it will be their best guide.

It is impossible to govern the world without the Bible.

—George Washington

The Bible is stamped with a specialty of origin, and an immeasurable distance separates it from all competitors.

—William E. Gladstone

The Bible is a Book of faith and a Book of doctrine, and a Book of religion, of special revelation from God.

—Daniel Webster

I will confess to you that the majesty of the Scriptures strikes me with admiration, as the purity of the gospel has its influence on my heart. Is it possible that a Book, at once so simple and so sublime, should be merely the work of a man?

—Jean Jacques Rousseau

In the Scriptures we have the only key that unlocks the mystery of the universe to man, and the mystery of man to himself.

—Ferrar Fenton

This Book is the one supreme source of revelation, the revelation of the meaning of life, the nature of God, and the spiritual nature and need of men. It is a Book which reveals every man to himself as a distinct moral agent, responsible not to men, not even to those men whom he has put over him in authority, but responsible through his own conscience to his Lord and Maker. Whenever a man sees this vision, he stands up a free man whatever may be the circumstances of his life.

—Woodrow Wilson

All the good from the Savior of the world is communicated to us through this Book. . . . All things most desirable for man's welfare, here and hereafter, are to be found portrayed in it.

—Abraham Lincoln

11 Peter

2 Grace and peace be multiplied unto you through the knowledge of God, and of Jesus our Lord,

3 According as his divine power hath given unto us all things that *pertain* unto life and godliness, through the knowledge of him that hath called us to glory and virtue:

4 Whereby are given unto us exceeding great and precious promises; that by these ye might be partakers of the divine nature, having escaped the corruption that is in the world through lust.

5 And besides this, giving all diligence, add to your faith virtue; and to virtue, knowledge;

6 And to knowledge, temperance; and to temperance, patience; and to patience, godliness;

7 And to godliness, brotherly kindness; and to brotherly kindness, charity.

8 For if these things be in you, and abound, they make *you that ye shall* neither *be* barren nor unfruitful in the knowledge of our Lord Jesus Christ.

9 But he that lacketh these things is blind, and cannot see afar off, and hath forgotten that he was purged from his old sins.

10 Wherefore the rather, brethren, give diligence to make your calling and election sure: for if ye do these things, ye shall never fall:

13 Yea, I think it meet, as long as I am in this tabernacle, to stir you up by putting *you* in remembrance;

14 Knowing that shortly I must put off *this* my tabernacle, even as our Lord Jesus Christ hath showed me.

15 Moreover I will endeavor that ye may be able after my decease to have these things always in remembrance.

16 For we have not followed cunningly devised fables, when we made known unto you the power and coming of our Lord Jesus Christ, but were eyewitnesses of his majesty.

17 For he received from God the Father honor and glory, when there came such a voice to him from the excellent glory, This is my beloved Son, in whom I am well pleased.

18 And this voice which came from heaven we heard, when we were with him in the holy mount.

19 We have also a more sure word of prophecy; whereunto ye do well that ye take heed, as unto a light that shineth in a dark place, until the day dawn, and the day-star arise in your hearts:

20 Knowing this first, that no prophecy of the Scripture is of any private interpretation.

21 For the prophecy came not in old time by the will of man: but holy men of God spake *as they were* moved by the Holy Ghost.

Listen to the Word of God—it was inspired by the Holy Spirit.

Reflections

God Is Love

The greatest happiness of life is the conviction that we are loved, loved for ourselves, or rather loved in spite of ourselves.

—Victor Hugo

Reach up as far as you can and God will reach down all the way.

—Vincent de Paul

You can trust the Man who died for you.

—Charles E. Cowman

Underlying everything was Christ's unswerving and rock-foundationed sureness that this world is God's world.

—Francis B. Sayre

He who thinks to reach God by running away from the world, when and where does he expect to meet Him?

—Rabindranath Tagore

If we could look steadily at the world and see it as it is in the eyes of God many of our estimates would be amazingly changed.

—Edward F. Garesche

The whole world is sustained by God's charity.

—The Talmud

What we love we grow to resemble.

—Bernard of Clairvaux

John

1 There was a man of the Pharisees, named Nicodemus, a ruler of the Jews:

2 The same came to Jesus by night, and said unto him, Rabbi, we know that thou art a teacher come from God: for no man can do these miracles that thou doest, except God be with him.

3 Jesus answered and said unto him, Verily, verily, I say unto thee, Except a man be born again, he cannot see the kingdom of God.

4 Nicodemus saith unto him, How can a man be born when he is old? can he enter the second time into his mother's womb, and be born?

5 Jesus answered, Verily, verily, I say unto thee, Except a man be born of water and *of* the Spirit, he cannot enter into the kingdom of God.

6 That which is born of the flesh is flesh; and that which is born of the Spirit is spirit.

7 Marvel not that I said unto thee, Ye must be born again.

8 The wind bloweth where it listeth, and thou hearest the sound thereof, but canst not tell whence it cometh, and whither it goeth: so is every one that is born of the Spirit.

9 Nicodemus answered and said unto him, How can these things be?

10 Jesus answered and said unto him, Art thou a master of Israel, and knowest not these things?

11 Verily, verily, I say unto thee, We speak that we do know, and testify that we have seen; and ye receive not our witness.

12 If I have told you earthly things, and ye believe not, how shall ye believe, if I tell you *of* heavenly things?

13 And no man hath ascended up to heaven, but he that came down from heaven, *even* the Son of man which is in heaven.

14 And as Moses lifted up the serpent in the wilderness, even so must the Son of man be lifted up:

15 That whosoever believeth in him should not perish, but have eternal life.

16 For God so loved the world, that he gave his only begotten Son, that whosoever believeth in him should not perish, but have everlasting life.

17 For God sent not his Son into the world to condemn the world; but that the world through him might be saved.

Just think of it—God loves the whole world!

No one can deal with the hearts of men unless he has the sympathy which is given by love. . . . You must have enough benevolence, not only for yourself, but for others, to pervade and fill them. This is what is meant by living a godly life.

—Henry Ward Beecher

Where there is love, there is concern. Where there is concern, there is kindness. Where there is kindness, there is harmony. Where there is harmony, there is helpfulness. Where there is helpfulness, there is Christ. Where there is Christ, there is love.

—William Arthur Ward

If a single man achieves the highest kind of love, it will be sufficient to neutralize the hate of millions.

—Mahatma Gandhi

A loving heart is the truest wisdom.

—Charles Dickens

All loves should simply be steppingstones to the love of God.

—Plato

It is possible that a man be so changed by love as hardly to be recognized as the same person.

—Terence

Love is an image of God, and not a lifeless image, but the living essence of the divine nature which beams full of all goodness.

—Martin Luther

John

33 Little children, yet a little while I am with you. Ye shall seek me; and as I said unto the Jews, Whither I go, ye cannot come; so now I say to you.

34 A new commandment I give unto you, That ye love one another; as I have loved you, that ye also love one another.

35 By this shall all *men* know that ye are my disciples, if ye have love one to another.

36 Simon Peter said unto him, Lord, whither goest thou? Jesus answered him, Whither I go, thou canst not follow me now; but thou shalt follow me afterwards.

37 Peter said unto him, Lord, why cannot I follow thee now? I will lay down my life for thy sake.

38 Jesus answered him. Wilt thou lay down thy life for my sake? Verily, verily, I say unto Thee, The cock shall not crow, till thou hast denied me thrice.

CHAPTER 14

1 Let not your heart be troubled: ye believe in God, believe also in me.

2 In my Father's house are many mansions: if *it were* not *so*, I would have told you. I go to prepare a place for you.

3 And if I go and prepare a place for you, I will come again, and receive you into myself; that where I am, *there* ye may be also.

4 And whither I go ye know, and the way ye know.

5 Thomas saith unto him, Lord, we know not whither thou goest; and how can we know the way?

6 Jesus saith unto him, I am the way, the truth, and the life: no man cometh unto the Father, but by me.

7 If ye had known me, ye should have known my Father also: and from henceforth ye know him, and have seen him.

8 Philip saith unto him, Lord, shew us the Father, and it sufficeth us.

9 Jesus saith unto him, Have I been so long time with you, and yet hast thou not known me, Philip? he that hath seen me hath seen the Father; and how sayest thou *then,* Shew us the Father?

10 Believest thou not that I am in the Father, and the Father in me? the words that I speak unto you I speak not of myself: but the Father that dwelleth in me, he doeth the works.

11 Believe me that I *am* in the Father, and the Father in me: or else believe me for the very works' sake.

12 Verily, verily, I say unto you, He that believeth on me, the works that I do shall he do also; and greater *works* than these shall he do; because I go unto my Father.

13 And whatsoever ye shall ask in my name, that will I do, that the Father may be glorified in the Son.

14 If ye shall ask any thing in my name, I will do *it*.

15 If ye love me, keep my commandments.

The mark of disciples of Christ is their love for one another.

Love is the weapon which Omnipotence reserved to conquer rebel man when all the rest had failed. Reason he parries; fear he answers blow for blow; future interest he meets with present pleasure; but love is that sun against whose melting beams the winter cannot stand. There is not one human being in a million, nor a thousand men in all earth's quintillion whose heart is hardened against love.

—*Charles Tupper*

Nor father or mother has loved you as God has, for it was that you might be happy when He gave His only Son. When He bowed His head in the death hour, love solemnized its triumph; the sacrifice there was completed.

—*Henry Wadsworth Longfellow*

If the tender, profound, and sympathizing love, practiced and recommended by Jesus, were paramount in every heart, the loftiest and most glorious idea of human society would be realized, and little be wanting to make this world a kingdom of heaven.

—*Friedrich Wilhelm Krummacher*

Could we with ink the oceans fill and were the skies of parchment made and every stalk on earth a quill and every man a scribe by trade, to write the love of God above would drain the oceans dry, nor could that scroll contain the whole though stretched from sky to sky.

—*Scribbled on an asylum wall*

Love all God's creation, both the whole and every grain of sand. Love every leaf, every ray of light. Love the animals, love the plants, love each separate thing. If you love each thing you will perceive the mystery of God in all; and when once you perceive this, you will thenceforward grow every day to a fuller understanding of it: until you come at last to love the whole world with a love that will be all-embracing and universal.

—*Feodor Dostoevski*

Romans

22 For we know that the whole creation groaneth and travaileth in pain together until now.

23 And not only *they*, but ourselves also, which have the firstfruits of the Spirit, even we ourselves groan within ourselves, waiting for the adoption, *to wit*, the redemption of our body.

24 For we are saved by hope: but hope that is seen is not hope: for what a man seeth, why doth he yet hope for?

25 But if we hope for that we see not, *then* do we with patience wait for it.

26 Likewise the Spirit also helpeth our infirmities: for we know not what we should pray for as we ought: but the Spirit itself maketh intercession for us with groanings which cannot be uttered.

27 And he that searcheth the hearts knoweth what *is* the mind of the Spirit, because he maketh intercession for the saints according to *the will of* God.

28 And we know that all things work together for good to them that love God, to them who are the called according to *his* purpose.

29 For whom he did foreknow, he also did predestinate *to be* conformed to the image of his Son, that he might be the firstborn among many brethren.

30 Moreover whom he did predestinate, them he also called: and whom he called, them he also justified: and whom he justified, them he also glorified.

31 What shall we then say to these things? If God *be* for us, who *can be* against us?

32 He that spared not his own Son, but delivered him up for us all, how shall he not with him also freely give us all things?

33 Who shall lay any thing to the charge of God's elect? *It is* God that justifieth.

34 Who *is* he that condemneth? *It is* Christ that died, yea rather, that is risen again, who is even at the right hand of God, who also maketh intercession for us.

35 Who shall separate us from the love of Christ? *shall* tribulation, or distress, or persecution, or famine, or nakedness, or peril, or sword?

36 As it is written, For thy sake we are killed all the day long; we are accounted as sheep for the slaughter.

37 Nay, in all these things we are more than conquerers through him that loved us.

38 For I am persuaded, that neither death, nor life, nor angels, nor principalities, nor powers, nor things present, nor things to come.

39 Nor height, nor depth, nor any other creature, shall be able to separate us from the love of God, which is in Christ Jesus our Lord.

Nothing can make God not love you.

The violence and evil of our time have been, when viewed collectively, the work of loveless men; impotent men who lust after sadistic power to conceal their failure as lovers; repressed and frustrated men, lamed by unloving parents and seeking revenge by taking refuge in a system of thought or a mode of life into which love cannot intrude. . . . Those who are impotent to love, from Hitler downward, must seek a negative counterpart in hatred and disintegration.

—Lewis Mumford

You cannot antagonize and influence at the same time.

—John Knox

He gives twice who gives quickly.

—Roman proverb

You must love the poor very much, or they will hate you for giving them bread.

—Vincent de Paul

Today Will Durant said that if he were beginning life again he would not plan to write twenty books, to achieve wealth or fame, but would try to live as nearly as he could in accordance with the teachings of Jesus Christ. He said, "I do not consider food, clothing, or luxuries important, but do consider living in accordance with the Golden Rule, not only the highest achievement but that which causes more happiness and satisfaction than any other way of life."

—Howard E. Kershner

In order to love people and to be loved by them, one must train oneself to gentleness, humility, the art of bearing with disagreeable people and things.

—Leo Tolstoy

Romans

1 I beseech you therefore, brethren, by the mercies of God, that ye present your bodies a living sacrifice, holy, acceptable unto God, *which* is your reasonable service.

2 And be not conformed to this world: but be ye transformed by the renewing of your mind, that ye may prove what *is* that good, and acceptable, and perfect, will of God.

3 For I say, through the grace given unto me, to every man that is among you, not to think *of himself* more highly than he ought to think; but to think soberly, according as God hath dealt to every man the measure of faith.

4 For as we have many members in one body, and all members have not the same office:

5 So we, *being* many, are one body in Christ, and every one members one of another.

6 Having then gifts differing according to the grace that is given to us, whether prophecy, *let us prophesy* according to the proportion of faith;

7 Or ministry, *let us wait* on *our* ministering: or he that teacheth, on teaching;

8 Or he that exhorteth, on exhortation: he that giveth, *let him do it* with simplicity; he that ruleth, with diligence; he that sheweth mercy, with cheerfulness.

9 *Let* love be without dissimulation. Abhor that which is evil; cleave to that which is good.

10 *Be* kindly affectioned one to another with brotherly love; in honour preferring one another;

11 Not slothful in business; fervent in spirit; serving the Lord;

12 Rejoicing in hope; patient in tribulation; continuing instant in prayer;

13 Distributing to the necessity of saints; given to hospitality.

14 Bless them which persecute you: bless, and curse not.

15 Rejoice with them that do rejoice, and weep with them that weep.

16 *Be* of the same mind one toward another. Mind not high things, but condescend to men of low estate. Be not wise in your own conceits.

17 Recompense to no man evil for evil. Provide things honest in the sight of all men.

18 If it be possible, as much as lieth in you, live peaceably with all men.

19 Dearly beloved, avenge not yourselves, but *rather* give place unto wrath: for it is written, Vengeance *is* mine; I will repay, saith the Lord.

20 Therefore if thine enemy hunger, feed him; if he thirst, give him drink: for in so doing thou shalt heap coals of fire on his head.

21 Be not overcome of evil, but overcome evil with good.

Love even your enemy.

All that is best in the civilization of today is the fruit of Christ's appearance among men.

—*Daniel Webster*

The man who knows best how to control his natural inclinations is more open to supernatural inspirations.

—*Jean Pierre Camus*

We are shaped and fashioned by what we love.

—*Goethe*

We owe to the Middle Ages the two worst inventions of humanity—romantic love and gunpowder.

—*Andrew Maurois*

One hour of love will teach a woman more of her true relations than all your philosophizing.

—*Margaret Fuller*

When a home is ruled according to God's Word, angels might be asked to stay with us, and they would not find themselves out of their element.

—*Charles Spurgeon*

God hath often a great share in a little home.

—*George Herbert*

Strength of character may be acquired at work, but beauty of character is learned at home.

—*Henry Drummond*

1 Corinthians

1 Though I speak with the tongues of men and of angels, and have not charity, I am become *as* sounding brass, or a tinkling cymbal.

2 And though I have *the gift of* prophecy, and understand all mysteries, and all knowledge; and though I have all faith, so that I could remove mountains, and have not charity, I am nothing.

3 And though I bestow all my goods to feed *the poor,* and though I give my body to be burned, and have not charity, it profiteth me nothing.

4 Charity suffereth long, *and* is kind; charity envieth not; charity vaunteth not itself, is not puffed up.

5 Doth not behave itself unseemly, seeketh not her own, is not easily provoked, thinketh no evil;

6 Rejoiceth not in iniquity, but rejoiceth in the truth;

7 Beareth all things, believeth all things, hopeth all things, endureth all things.

8 Charity never faileth; but whether *there be* prophecies, they shall fail; whether *there be* tongues, they shall cease; whether *there be* knowledge, it shall vanish away.

9 For we know in part, and we prophesy in part.

10 But when that which is perfect is come, then that which is in part shall be done away.

11 When I was a child, I spake as a child, I understood as a child, I thought as a child: but when I became a man, I put away childish things.

12 For now we see through a glass, darkly, but then face to face: now I know in part; but then shall I know even as also I am known.

13 And now abideth faith, hope, charity, these three; but the greatest of these *is* charity.

Make love your aim.

The more one judges, the less one loves.

—*Honoré de Balzac*

The Christian cannot promise to do or not to do a given thing at a given time, for he cannot know what the law of love, which is the commanding principle of his life, will demand of him at that time.

—*Leo Tolstoy*

We are all born for love. It is the principle of existence, and its only end.

—*Benjamin Disraeli*

An hour spent in hate is an eternity withdrawn from love.

—*Ludwig Boerne*

Heaven does not open its door to those who hate.

—*B. W. Maturin*

We may fight against what is wrong, but if we allow ourselves to hate, that is to insure our spiritual defeat and our likeness to what we hate.

—*George William Russell*

Hating people is like burning down your house to get rid of a rat.

—*Harry Emerson Fosdick*

It is the duty of men to love even those who injure them.

—*Marcus Antoninus*

1 John

9 He that saith he is in the light, and hateth his brother, is in darkness even until now.

10 He that loveth his brother abideth in the light, and there is none occasion of stumbling in him.

11 But he that hateth his brother is in darkness, and walketh in darkness, and knoweth not whither he goeth, because that darkness hath blinded his eyes.

15 Love not the world, neither the things *that are* in the world. If any man love the world, the love of the Father is not in him.

16 For all that *is* in the world, the lust of the flesh, and the lust of the eyes, and the pride of life, is not of the Father, but is of the world.

17 And the world passeth away, and the lust thereof: but he that doeth the will of God abideth for ever.

CHAPTER 3

1 Behold, what manner of love the Father hath bestowed upon us, that we should be called the sons of God: therefore the world knoweth us not, because it knew him not.

2 Beloved, now are we the sons of God, and it doth not yet appear what we shall be: but we know that, when he shall appear, we shall be like him; for we shall see him as he is.

3 And every man that hath this hope in him purifieth himself, even as he is pure.

4 Whosoever committeth sin transgresseth also the law: for sin is the transgression of the law.

5 And ye know that he was manifested to take away our sins; and in him is no sin.

10 In this the children of God are manifest, and the children of the devil: whosoever doeth not righteousness is not of God, neither he that loveth not his brother.

11 For this is the message that ye heard from the beginning, that we should love one another.

12 Not as Cain, *who* was of that wicked one, and slew his brother. And wherefore slew he him? Because his own works were evil, and his brother's righteous.

13 Marvel not, my brethren, if the world hate you.

14 We know that we have passed from death unto life, because we love the brethren. He that loveth not *his* brother abideth in death.

15 Whosoever hateth his brother is a murderer: and ye know that no murderer hath eternal life abiding in him.

16 Hereby perceive we the love *of God,* because he laid down his life for us: and we ought to lay down *our* lives for the brethren.

17 But whoso hath this world's good, and seeth his brother have need, and shutteth up his bowels *of compassion* from him, how dwelleth the love of God in him?

18 My little children, let us not love in word, neither in tongue; but in deed and in truth.

Love those who are difficult to love.

You will find as you look back on your life that the moments that stand out above everything else are the moments when you have done things in a spirit of love.

—*Henry Drummond*

To love someone means to see him as God intended him.

—*Feodor Dostoevski*

We praise those who love their fellow men.

—*Aristotle*

The true measure of loving God is to love Him without measure.

—*Bernard of Clairvaux*

It is the very essence of love, of nobleness, of greatness to be willing to suffer for the good of others.

—*Spence*

He that strives to draw himself from obedience, withdraws himself from grace.

—*Thomas à Kempis*

All the things that God would have us to do are hard for us to do—remember that—and hence, He oftener commands us than endeavors to persuade. And if we obey God, we must disobey ourselves, wherein the hardness of obeying God consists.

—*Herman Melville*

You will give us joy and gladness if you obey what we have written through the Holy Spirit.

—*Clement of Rome*

1 John

7 Beloved, let us love one another: for love is of God; and every one that loveth is born of God, and knoweth God.

8 He that loveth not knoweth not God; for God is love.

9 In this was manifested the love of God toward us, because that God sent his only begotten Son into the world, that we might live through him.

10 Herein is love, not that we loved God, but that he loved us, and sent his Son *to be* the propitiation for our sins.

11 Beloved, if God so loved us, we ought also to love one another.

12 No man hath seen God at any time. If we love one another, God dwelleth in us, and his love is perfected in us.

13 Hereby know we that we dwell in him, and he in us, because he has given us of his Spirit.

14 And we have seen and do testify that the Father sent the Son *to be* the Saviour of the world.

15 Whosoever shall confess that Jesus is the Son of God, God dwelleth in him, and he in God.

16 And we have known and believed the love that God hath to us. God is love; and he that dwelleth in love dwelleth in God, and God in him.

17 Herein is our love made perfect, that we may have boldness in the day of judgment: because as he is, so are we in this world.

18 There is no fear in love; but perfect love casteth out fear: because fear hath torment. He that feareth is not made perfect in love.

19 We love him, because he first loved us.

20 If a man say, I love God, and hateth his brother, he is a liar: for he that loveth not his brother whom he hath seen, how can he love God whom he hath not seen?

21 And this commandment have we from him, That he who loveth God love his brother also.

CHAPTER 5

1 Whosoever believeth that Jesus is the Christ is born of God: and every one that loveth him that begat loveth him also that is begotten of him.

2 By this we know that we love the children of God, when we love God, and keep his commandments.

3 For this is the love of God, that we keep his commandments: and his commandments are not grievous.

To God, love is evident in obedience.

Reflections

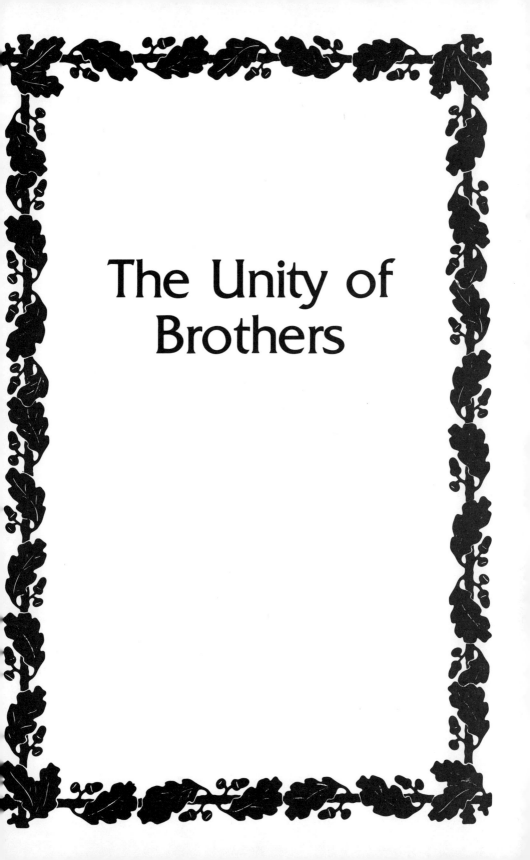

The Unity of Brothers

Brothers on mission forming small radiants of light are bearers of Christ simply by their presence. Without knowing how, through this simple Christ-like presence, God assures and transfigures this world slow to believe.

—Rule of Taize

Behold how good and how pleasant it is for brethren to dwell together in unity.

—Psalm 133:1

Be a ferment of unity.

—Rule of Taize

We must not only affirm the brotherhood of man; we must live it.

—Henry Codman Potter

Honor all men; love the brotherhood.

— 1 Peter 2:17

Affliction's sons are brothers in distress:
A brother to relieve—how exquisite the bliss!

—Robert Burns

Many great political thinkers through the centuries in various cultures have recognized that if man is to really understand his personal relationship to others he must have an allegiance beyond ego. We are all born with ego; some of us control it and others don't, depending on our priorities, values, and commitments. I do not believe that this nation or any other can sever its roots from what I call "things of the spirit" and remain strong. The only way we can sense a true brotherhood and reach out in compassion to communicate with others . . . is through this spiritual nature within us.

—Mark O. Hatfield

1 Samuel

1 And it came to pass, when he had made an end of speaking unto Saul, that the soul of Jonathan was knit with the soul of David, and Jonathan loved him as his own soul.

2 And Saul took him that day, and would let him go no more home to his father's house.

3 Then Jonathan and David made a covenant, because he loved him as his own soul.

4 And Jonathan stripped himself of the robe that *was* upon him, and gave it to David, and his garments, even to his sword, and to his bow, and to his girdle.

5 And David went out whithersoever Saul sent him, *and* behaved himself wisely: and Saul set him over the men of war, and he was accepted in the sight of all the people, and also in the sight of Saul's servants.

6 And it came to pass as they came, when David was returned from the slaughter of the Philistine, that the women came out of all cities of Israel, singing and dancing, to meet king Saul, with tabrets, with joy, and with instruments of music.

7 And the women answered *one another* as they played, and said, Saul hath slain his thousands, and David his ten thousands.

8 And Saul was very wroth, and the saying displeased him; and he said, They have ascribed unto David ten thousands, and to me they have ascribed *but* thousands: and *what* can he have more but the kingdom?

9 And Saul eyed David from that day and forward.

CHAPTER 20

11 And Jonathan said unto David, Come, and let us go out into the field. And they went out both of them into the field.

12 And Jonathan said unto David, O Lord God of Israel, when I have sounded my father about tomorrow any time, *or* the third *day,* and, behold, *if there be* good toward David, and I then send not unto thee, and show it thee;

13 The Lord do so and much more to Jonathan: but if it please my father *to do* thee evil, then I will show it thee, and send thee away, that thou mayest go in peace: and the Lord be with thee, as he hath been with my father.

14 And thou shalt not only while yet I live show me the kindness of the Lord, that I die not:

15 But *also* thou shalt not cut off thy kindness from my house for ever: no, not when the Lord hath cut off the enemies of David every one from the face of the earth.

16 So Jonathan made a *covenant* with the house of David, *saying,* Let the Lord even require *it* at the hand of David's enemies.

17 And Jonathan caused David to swear again, because he loved him: for he loved him as he loved his own soul.

Jonathan and David had a bond that blessed the whole nation.

He has the right to criticize who has a heart to help.

—Abraham Lincoln

It is one of the severest tests of friendship to tell your friend his faults. So to love a man that you cannot bear to see a stain on him, and to speak painful truth through loving words, that is friendship.

—Henry Ward Beecher

Settle one difficulty and you keep a hundred others away.

—Unknown

The people to fear are not those who disagree with you but those who disagree with you and are too cowardly to let you know.

—Napoléon Bonaparte

Little, vicious minds abound with anger and revenge, and are incapable of feeling the pleasure of forgiving their enemies.

—Philip, Earl of Chesterfield

He who forgives ends the quarrel.

—Unknown

I sought my soul—but my soul I could not see; I sought my God—but my God eluded me; I sought my brother—and found all three.

—Unknown

The perfect friendship is that between good men, alike in their virtue.

—Aristotle

Matthew

15 Moreover if thy brother shall trespass against thee, go and tell him his fault between thee and him alone: if he shall hear thee, thou hast gained thy brother.

16 But if he will not hear *thee, then* take with thee one or two more, that in the mouth of two or three witnesses every word may be established.

17 And if he shall neglect to hear them, tell *it* unto the church: but if he neglect to hear the church, let him be unto thee as a heathen man and a publican.

19 Again I say unto you, That if two of you shall agree on earth as touching any thing that they shall ask, it shall be done for them of my Father which is in heaven.

20 For where two or three are gathered together in my name, there am I in the midst of them.

21 Then came Peter to him, and said, Lord, how oft shall my brother sin against me, and I forgive him? till seven times?

22 Jesus saith unto him, I say not unto thee, Until seven times: but, Until seventy times seven.

23 Therefore is the kingdom of heaven likened unto a certain king, which would take account of his servants.

24 And when he had begun to reckon, one was brought unto him, which owed him ten thousand talents.

25 But forasmuch as he had not to pay, his lord commanded him to be sold, and his wife, and children, and all that he had, and payment to be made.

26 The servant therefore fell down, and worshipped him, saying, Lord, have patience with me, and I will pay thee all.

27 Then the lord of that servant was moved with compassion, and loosed him, and forgave him the debt.

28 But the same servant went out, and found one of his fellow servants, which owed him a hundred pence: and he laid hands on him, and took *him* by the throat, saying, Pay me that thou owest.

29 And his fellow servant fell down at his feet, and besought him, saying, Have patience with me, and I will pay thee all.

30 And he would not: but went and cast him into prison, till he should pay the debt.

31 So when his fellow servants saw what was done, they were very sorry, and came and told unto their lord all that was done.

32 Then his lord, after that he had called him, said unto him, O thou wicked servant, I forgave thee all that debt, because thou desiredst me:

33 Shouldest not thou also have had compassion on thy fellow servant, even as I had pity on thee?

34 And his lord was wroth, and delivered him to the tormentors, till he should pay all that was due unto him.

35 So likewise shall my heavenly Father do also unto you, if ye from your hearts forgive not every one his brother their trespasses.

Contemplate the potential influence of two or three men bound together in Jesus Christ.

And they, continuing daily with one accord in the temple, and breaking bread from house to house, did eat their meat with gladness and singleness of heart, Praising God, and having favor with all the people. . . .

—Acts 2:46, 47

We live for others in the inevitable conditions of our being. To accept the situation gladly is to find it crowned with its own joy.

—Unknown

The greatest difficulty with the world is not its inability to produce, but its unwillingness to share.

—Roy L. Smith

If a man says, I love God, and hateth his brother, he is a lair. . . .

—1 John 4:20

Reach that which is of God in everyone.

—George Fox

Blow wind of God and set us free from hate and want of charity; Strip off the trappings of our pride, and give us to our brother's side.

—W. C. Braithwaite

We know that we have passed from death unto life because we love the brethren. . . .

—1 John 3:14

John

1 These words spake Jesus, and lifted up his eyes to heaven, and said, Father, the hour is come; glorify thy Son, that thy Son also may glorify thee:

2 As thou hast given him power over all flesh, that he should give eternal life to as many as thou hast given him.

3 And this is life eternal, that they might know thee the only true God, and Jesus Christ, whom thou hast sent.

4 I have glorified thee on the earth: I have finished the work which thou gavest me to do.

5 And now, O Father, glorify thou me with thine own self with the glory which I had with thee before the world was.

6 I have manifested thy name unto the men which thou gavest me out of the world: thine they were, and thou gavest them me; and they have kept thy word.

7 Now they have known that all things whatsoever thou hast given me are of thee.

8 For I have given unto them the words which thou gavest me; and they have received *them,* and have known surely that I came out from thee, and they have believed that thou didst send me.

9 I pray for them: I pray not for the world, but for them which thou hast given me; for they are thine.

10 And all mine are thine, and thine are mine; and I am glorified in them.

11 And now I am no more in the world, but these are in the world, and I come to thee. Holy Father, keep through thine own name those whom thou hast given me, and they may be one, as we *are.*

12 While I was with them in the world, I kept them in thy name: those that thou gavest me I have kept, and none of them is lost, but the son of perdition; that the Scripture might be fulfilled

13 And now come I to thee; and these things I speak in the world, that they might have my joy fulfilled in themselves.

14 I have given them thy word; and the world hath hated them, because they are not of the world, even as I am not of the world.

15 I pray not that thou shouldest take them out of the world, but that thou shouldest keep them from the evil.

16 They are not of the world, even as I am not of the world.

17 Sanctify them through thy truth: thy word is truth.

18 As thou hast sent me into the world, even so have I also sent them into the world.

19 And for their sakes I sanctify myself, that they also might be sanctified through the truth.

20 Neither pray I for these alone, but for them also which shall believe on me through their word;

21 That they all may be one; as thou, Father, *are* in me, and I in thee, that they also may be one in us: that the world may believe that thou hast sent me.

God's plan is the unity of brothers.

When John Wesley was first converted he retired from the world to study. One day an old man said to him: "Sir, if you wish to serve God, you can't serve Him alone. You must find companions or make them. The Bible knows nothing of solitary religion." From that day, John Wesley's fellowship warmed all England.

—Robert D. Hershey

Gold is tried in fire, and acceptable men in the furnace of adversity.

—Seneca

The unlearned rise and take heaven itself by storm.

—Augustine

Yes, we must indeed all hang together, or most assuredly, we shall all hang separately.

—Benjamin Franklin

As the Father hath loved me, so have I loved you: continue ye in my love. . . . This is my commandment, That ye love one another, as I have loved you. Greater love hath no man than this, that a man lay down his life for his friends.

—John 15:9–13

Blessed are they who have the gift of making friends, for it is one of God's best gifts. It involves many things, but above all, the power of going out of one's self, and appreciating whatever is noble and loving in another.

—Thomas Hughes

Arts

8 Then Peter, filled with the Holy Ghost, said unto them, Ye rulers of the people, and elders of Israel,

9 If we this day be examined of the good deed done to the impotent man, by what means he is made whole;

10 Be it known unto you all, and to all the people of Israel, that by the name of Jesus Christ of Nazareth, whom ye crucified, whom God raised from the dead, *even* by him doth this man stand here before you whole.

14 And beholding the man which was healed standing with them, they could say nothing against it.

18 And they called them, and commanded them not to speak at all nor teach in the name of Jesus.

19 But Peter and John answered and said unto them, Whether it be right in the sight of God to hearken unto you more than unto God, judge ye.

20 For we cannot but speak the things which we have seen and heard.

23 And being let go, they went to their own company, and reported all that the chief priests and elders had said unto them.

24 And when they heard that, they lifted up their voice to God with one accord, and said, Lord, thou *art* God, which hast made heaven, and earth, and the sea, and all that in them is;

25 Who by the mouth of thy servant David hast said, Why did the heathen rage, and the people imagine vain things?

26 The kings of the earth stood up, and the rulers were gathered together against the Lord, and against his Christ.

27 For of a truth against thy holy child Jesus, whom thou hast anointed, both Herod, and Pontius Pilate, with the Gentiles, and the people of Israel, were gathered together,

28 For to do whatsoever thy hand and thy counsel determined before to be done.

29 And now, Lord, behold their threatenings: and grant unto thy servants, that with all boldness they may speak thy word,

30 By stretching forth thine hand to heal; and that signs and wonders may be done by the name of thy holy child Jesus.

31 And when they had prayed, the place was shaken where they were assembled together; and they were all filled with the Holy Ghost, and they spake the word of God with boldness.

32 And the multitude of them that believed were of one heart and of one soul: neither said any *of them* that aught of the things which he possessed was his own; but they had all things common.

There is a genuine excitement in being part of a group of friends who are of one mind and heart.

In essentials unity, in nonessentials liberty, in all things charity.

—Augustine

Difference of opinion was never, with me, a motive of separation from a friend.

—Thomas Jefferson

To be able to argue, men must first understand each other.

—Honoré de Balzac

Honest differences of views and honest debate are not disunity. They are the vital process of policy-making among free men.

—Herbert Hoover

Loyalty to petrified opinion never yet broke a chain or freed a human soul.

—Mark Twain

You can't hold a man down without staying down with him.

—Booker T. Washington

Men exist for the sake of one another. Teach them then or bear with them.

—Edwin Arnold

Romans

1 Him that is weak in the faith receive ye, *but* not to doubtful disputations.

2 For one believeth that he may eat all things: another, who is weak, eateth herbs.

3 Let not him that eateth despise him that eateth not; and let not him which eateth not judge him that eateth: for God hath received him.

13 Let us not therefore judge one another any more: but judge this rather, that no man put a stumblingblock or an occasion to fall in *his* brother's way.

14 I know, and am persuaded by the Lord Jesus, that *there is* nothing unclean of itself: but to him that esteemeth any thing to be unclean, to him *it is* unclean.

15 But if thy brother be grieved with *thy* meat, now walkest thou not charitably. Destroy not him with thy meat, for whom Christ died.

16 Let not then your good be evil spoken of:

17 For the kingdom of God is not meat and drink; but righteousness, and peace, and joy in the Holy Ghost.

18 For he that in these things serveth Christ *is* acceptable to God, and approved of men.

19 Let us therefore follow after the things which make for peace, and things wherewith one may edify another.

20 For meat destroy not the work of God. All things indeed *are* pure; but *it is* evil for that man who eateth with offense.

21 *It is* good neither to eat flesh, nor to drink wine, nor *any thing* whereby thy brother stumbleth, or is offended, or is made weak.

22 Hast thou faith: have *it* to thyself before God. Happy *is* he that condemneth not himself in that thing which he alloweth.

23 And he that doubteth is damned if he eat, because *he eateth* not of faith: for whatsoever *is* not of faith is sin.

CHAPER 15

1 We then that are strong ought to bear the infirmities of the weak, and not to please ourselves.

2 Let every one of us please *his* neighbor for *his* good to edification.

3 For even Christ pleased not himself; but, as it is written, The reproaches of them that reproached thee fell on me.

4 For whatsoever things were written aforetime were written for our learning, that we through patience and comfort of the Scriptures might have hope.

5 Now the God of patience and consolation grant you to be likeminded one toward another according to Christ Jesus:

6 That ye may with one mind *and* one mouth glorify God, even the Father of our Lord Jesus Christ.

7 Wherefore receive ye one another, as Christ also received us, to the glory of God.

Live in harmony with your friends. It glorifies God.

The leader's flame that burns so bright in battle is not his alone. It comes from the interplay of his forces and those of the members of the team. Both contribute essentials which produce leadership.

—*Matthew Ridgway*

It has been said that we feed the hungry, clothe the naked, bind up the wounds of the man beaten by thieves, pour oil and wine into them, set him on our own beast and bring him to the inn, because we receive ourselves pleasure from these acts. . . . This indeed is true. But it is one step short of the ultimate question. Nature hath implanted in our breasts a love of others, a sense of duty to them, a moral instinct, in short, which prompts us irresistibly to feel and to succor their distresses.

—*Thomas Jefferson*

Light is the task when many share the toil.

—*Homer*

The multitude which does not reduce itself to unity is confusion; the unity which does not depend upon the multitude, is tyranny.

—*Blaise Pascal*

We cannot hope to command brotherhood abroad unless we practice it at home.

—*Harry Truman*

Two are better than one; because they have a good reward for their labor. For if they fall, the one will lift up his fellow: but woe to him that is alone when he falleth; for he hath not another to help him up. . . . And if one prevail against him, two shall withstand him; and a threefold cord is not quickly broken.

—*Ecclesiastes 4:9,10,12*

1 Corinthians

1 Now concerning spiritual *gifts*, brethren, I would not have you ignorant.

2 Ye know that ye were Gentiles, carried away unto these dumb idols, even as ye were led.

3 Wherefore I give you to understand, that no man speaking by the Spirit of God calleth Jesus accursed: and *that* no man can say that Jesus is the Lord, but by the Holy Ghost.

4 Now there are diversities of gifts, but the same Spirit.

5 And there are differences of administrations, but the same Lord.

6 And there are diversities of operations, but it is the same God which worketh all in all.

7 But the manifestation of the Spirit is given to every man to profit withal.

8 For to one is given by the Spirit the word of wisdom; to another the word of knowledge by the same Spirit;

9 To another faith by the same Spirit; to another the gifts of healing by the same Spirit;

10 To another the working of miracles; to another prophecy; to another discerning of spirits; to another *divers* kinds of tongues; to another the interpretation of tongues:

11 But all these worketh that one and the selfsame Spirit, dividing to every man severally as he will.

12 For as the body is one, and hath many members and all the members of that one body, being many, are one body: so also *is* Christ.

13 For by one Spirit are we all baptized into one body, whether *we be* Jews or Gentiles, whether *we be* bond or free; and have been all made to drink into one Spirit.

14 For the body is not one member, but many.

17 If the whole body *were* an eye, where *were* the hearing? If the whole *were* hearing, where *were* the smelling?

18 But now hath God set the members every one of them in the body, as it hath pleased him.

19 And if they were all one member, where *were* the body?

20 But now *are they* many members, yet but one body.

23 And those *members* of the body, which we think to be less honorable, upon these we bestow more abundant honor; and our uncomely *parts* have more abundant comeliness.

24 For our comely *parts* have no need: but God hath tempered the body together, having given more abundant honor to that *part* which lacked:

25 That there should be no schism in the body; but *that* the members should have the same care one for another.

26 And whether one member suffer, all the members suffer with it; or one member be honored, all the members rejoice with it.

We have different capacities, but the same Spirit keeps us together.

The race of mankind would perish from the earth did they cease to aid each other.

—*Sir Walter Scott*

Cooperation is spelled with two letters—WE.

—*G. M. Verity*

When men come face to face, their differences often vanish.

—*Unknown*

There is a law that man should love his neighbor as himself. In a few hundred years it should be as natural to mankind as breathing or the upright gait; but if he does not learn it he must perish.

—*Alfred Adler*

God divided man into men, that they might help each other.

—*Seneca*

Of a truth men are mystically united; a mysterious bond of brotherhood makes all men one.

—*Thomas Carlyle*

We force no doors in friendship, but like the Christ in Revelation, we stand reverently at the door without, to knock. And only if the door be opened from within, may we welcome in to sup with our friend and he with us. The glory of friendship is not the outstretched hand, nor the kindly smile, nor the joy of companionship; it is the spiritual inspiration that comes to one when he discovers that someone else believes in him and is willing to trust him with his friendship. My friends have come unsought. The great God gave them to me.

—*Ralph Waldo Emerson*

Ephesians

1 I therefore, the prisoner of the Lord, beseech you that ye walk worthy of the vocation wherewith ye are called,

2 With all lowliness and meekness, with longsuffering, forbearing one another in love;

3 Endeavouring to keep the unity of the Spirit in the bond of peace.

4 *There is* one body, and one Spirit, even as ye are called in one hope of your calling;

5 One Lord, one faith, one baptism,

6 One God and Father of all, who *is* above all, and through all, and in you all.

7 But unto every one of us is given grace according to the measure of the gift of Christ.

8 Wherefore he saith, When he ascended up on high, he led captivity captive, and gave gifts unto men.

9 (Now that he ascended, what is it but that he also descended first into the lower parts of the earth?

10 He that descended is the same also that ascended up far above all heavens, that he might fill all things.)

11 And he gave some, apostles; and some, prophets; and some, evangelists; and some, pastors and teachers;

12 For the perfecting of the saints, for the work of the ministry, for the edifying of the body of Christ:

13 Till we all come in the unity of the faith, and of the knowledge of the Son of God, unto a perfect man, unto the measure of the stature of the fulness of Christ:

14 That we *henceforth* be no more children, tossed to and fro, and carried about with every wind of doctrine, by the sleight of men, *and* cunning craftiness, whereby they lie in wait to deceive;

15 But speaking the truth in love, may grow up into him in all things, which is the head, *even* Christ:

16 From whom the whole body fitly joined together and compacted by that which every joint supplieth, according to the effectual working in the measure of every part, maketh increase of the body unto the edifying of itself in love.

Are you of one mind and one spirit with anyone?

The belief of a God, so far from having anything of mystery in it, is of all beliefs the most easy, because it arises to us, as is before observed, out of necessity. And the practice of moral truth, or, in other words, a practical imitation of the moral goodness of God, is no other than our acting towards each other as He acts benignly towards all. We cannot serve God in the manner we serve those who cannot do without such service; and therefore, the only idea we can have of serving God is that of contributing to the happiness of the living creation that God has made. This cannot be done by retiring ourselves from the society of the world, and spending a recluse life in selfish devotion.

—Thomas Paine

Men cannot be brothers if they are not humble. It is pride, no matter how legitimate it may seem to be, which provokes tension and struggles for prestige, for predominance, colonialism, egosim. That is, pride disrupts brotherhood.

—Pope Paul VI

Competition, founded upon the conflicting interests of individuals, is in reality far less productive of wealth and enterprise than cooperation, involving though it does the constant apparent sacrifice of the individual to the common interests.

—R. H. Benson

"A friend is the one who comes in when the whole world has gone out." Even as David thanked God for Jonathan and praised him in well-remembered lines, so have we abundant reasons to thank God today for friends and to resolve to keep these friendships in constant repair.

—Edgar DeWitt Jones

1 Peter

1 Likewise, ye wives, *be* in subjection to your own husbands; that, if any obey not the word, they also may without the word be won by the conversation of the wives;

2 While they behold your chaste conversation *coupled* with fear.

3 Whose adorning, let it not be that outward *adorning* of plaiting the hair, and of wearing of gold, or of putting on of apparel;

4 But *let it be* the hidden man of the heart, in that which is not corruptible, *even the ornament* of a meek and quiet spirit, which is in the sight of God of great price.

5 For after this manner in the old time the holy women also, who trusted in God, adorned themselves, being in subjection unto their own husbands:

6 Even as Sarah obeyed Abraham, calling him lord: whose daughters ye are, as long as ye do well, and are not afraid with any amazement.

7 Likewise, ye husbands, dwell with *them* according to knowledge, giving honour unto the wife, as unto the weaker vessel, and as being heirs together of the grace of life; that your prayers be not hindered.

8 Finally, *be ye* all of one mind, having compassion one of another; love as brethren, *be* pitiful, *be* courteous:

9 Not rendering evil for evil, or railing for railing: but contrariwise blessing; knowing that ye are thereunto called, that ye should inherit a blessing.

10 For he that will love life, and see good days, let him refrain his tongue from evil, and his lips that they speak no guile:

11 Let him eschew evil, and do good; let him seek peace, and ensue it.

12 For the eyes of the Lord *are* over the righteous, and his ears *are open* unto their prayers: but the face of the Lord *is* against them that do evil.

13 And who *is* he that will harm you, if ye be followers of that which is good?

14 But and if ye suffer for righteousness' sake, happy *are ye:* and be not afraid of their terror, neither be troubled;

15 But sanctify the Lord God in your hearts: and *be* ready always to *give* an answer to every man that asketh you a reason of the hope that is in you, with meekness and fear:

16 Having a good conscience; that, whereas they speak evil of you, as of evil doers, they may be ashamed that falsely accuse your good conversation in Christ.

17 For *it* is better, if the will of God be so, that ye suffer for well doing, than for evil doing.

18 For Christ also hath once suffered for sins, the just for the unjust, that he might bring us to God, being put to death in the flesh, but quickened by the Spirit.

Jesus Christ can keep your family and friends together.

Reflections

The Royal Law —
Care for Others

The practical weakness of the vast mass of modern pity for the poor and the oppressed is precisely that it is merely pity; the pity is pitiful but not respectful. Men feel that the cruelty to the poor is a kind of cruelty to animals. They never feel that it is injustice to equals; nay it is treachery to comrades.

—Gilbert Keith Chesterton

For it is written by the finger of the Almighty in the everlasting tablets of the universe that no nation can endure and prosper into and through whose life does not run the golden thread of equal, exact, and universal justice.

—David Josiah Brewer

The most acceptable service of God is doing good to man.

—Benjamin Franklin

God gives manhood but one clue to success, utter and exact justice; that, He guarantees, shall be always expediency.

—Wendell Phillips

The mistake of the best men through generation after generation has been the great one of thinking to help the poor by almsgiving, and by preaching of patience or of hope, and by every other means, emollient or consolatory, except the one thing which God orders for them, justice.

—John Ruskin

The highest of distinctions is the service of others.

—King George VI

Psalms

1 Give the king thy judgments, O God, and thy righteousness unto the king's son.

2 He shall judge thy people with righteousness, and thy poor with judgment.

3 The mountains shall bring peace to the people, and the little hills, by righteousness.

4 He shall judge the poor of the people, he shall save the children of the needy, and shall break in pieces the oppressor.

5 They shall fear thee as long as the sun and moon endure, throughout all generations.

6 He shall come down like rain upon the mown grass: as showers *that* water the earth.

7 In his days shall the righteous flourish; and abundance of peace so long as the moon endureth.

8 He shall have dominion also from sea to sea, and from the river unto the ends of the earth.

9 They that dwell in the wilderness shall bow before him; and his enemies shall lick the dust.

10 The kings of Tarshish and of the isles shall bring presents: the kings of Sheba and Seba shall offer gifts.

11 Yea, all kings shall fall down before him: and nations shall serve him.

12 For he shall deliver the needy when he crieth; the poor also, and *him* that hath no helper.

13 He shall spare the poor and needy, and shall save the souls of the needy.

14 He shall redeem their soul from deceit and violence: and precious shall their blood be in his sight.

15 And he shall live, and to him shall be given of the gold of Sheba: prayer also shall be made for him continually; *and* daily shall he be praised.

16 There shall be a handful of corn in the earth upon the top of the mountains; the fruit thereof shall shake like Lebanon: and *they* of the city shall flourish like grass of the earth.

17 His name shall endure for ever: his name shall be continued as long as the sun: and *men* shall be blessed in him: all nations shall call him blessed.

18 Blessed *be* the Lord God, the God of Israel, who only doeth wondrous things.

19 And blessed *be* his glorious name for ever: and let the whole earth be filled *with* his glory. Amen, and Amen.

God is a champion of justice, and so should be those who follow Him.

Of more worth is one honest man to society, and in the sight of God, than all the crowned ruffians that ever lived.

—Thomas Paine

Resistance to tyrants is obedience to God.

—Thomas Jefferson

Delight, top-gallant delight, is to him who acknowledges no law or lord but the Lord his God, and is only patriot to heaven.

—Herman Melville

The world is weary of the church that keeps silent on the issues of life.

—Edwin T. Dahlberg

O ye that love mankind! Yes that dare oppose not only tyranny but the tyrant, stand forth!

—Thomas Paine

The worst sin towards our fellow creatures is not to hate them, but to be indifferent to them: that's the essence of inhumanity.

—George Bernard Shaw

Wherever there is a human being, I see God-given rights inherent in that being, whatever may be the sex or complexion.

—William Lloyd Garrison

Psalms

1 Praise ye the LORD. Praise the LORD, O my soul.

2 While I live will I praise the LORD: I will sing praises unto my God while I have any being.

3 Put not your trust in princes, *nor* in the son of man, in whom *there is* no help.

4 His breath goeth forth, he returneth to his earth; in that very day his thoughts perish.

5 Happy *is he* that *hath* the God of Jacob for his help, whose hope *is* in the LORD his God:

6 Which made heaven, and earth, the sea, and all that therein *is:* which keepeth truth for ever:

7 Which executeth judgment for the oppressed: which giveth food to the hungry. The LORD looseth the prisoners:

8 The LORD openeth the *eyes of* the blind: the LORD raiseth them that are bowed down: the LORD loveth the righteous:

9 The LORD preserveth the strangers; he relieveth the fatherless and widow: but the way of the wicked he turneth upside down.

10 The LORD shall reign for ever, *even* thy God, O Zion, unto all generations. Praise ye the LORD.

The oppressed, the hungry, the blind, the lonely— the Lord has not forgotten them, nor should we.

Whoever is spared personal pain must feel himself called to help in diminishing the pain of others. We must all carry our share of the misery which lies upon the world.

—Albert Schweitzer

Why not give Christ's way a trial? The question seems a hopeless one after two thousand years of resolute adherence to the old cry of "Not this man, but Barrabas." "This man" has not been a failure yet, for nobody has ever been sane enough to try His way.

—George Bernard Shaw

While there is a lower class, I am in it. While there is a criminal class, I am of it. While there is a soul in prison, I am not free.

—Eugene V. Debs

Compassion is the basis of all morality.

—Arthur Schopenhauer

Morality, said Jesus, is kindness to the weak; morality, said Nietzsche, is the bravery of the strong; morality, said Plato, is the effective harmony of the whole. Probably all three doctrines must be combined to find a perfect ethic; but can we doubt which of the elements is fundamental?

—Will Durant

Neither genius, fame, nor love show the greatness of the soul. Only kindness can do that.

—Jean Baptiste Henri Lacordaire

Isaiah

1 Cry aloud, spare not, lift up thy voice like a trumpet, and show my people their transgression, and the house of Jacob their sins.

2 Yet they seek me daily, and delight to know my ways, as a nation that did righteousness, and forsook not the ordinance of their God: they ask of me the ordinances of justice; they take delight in approaching to God.

3 Wherefore have we fasted, *say they*, and thou seest not? *wherefore* have we afflicted our soul, and thou takest not knowledge? Behold, in the day of your fast ye find pleasure, and exact all your labors.

4 Behold, ye fast for strife and debate, and to smite with the fist of wickedness: ye shall not fast as *ye do this* day, to make your voice to be heard on high.

6 *Is* not this the fast that I have chosen? to loose the bands of wickedness, to undo the heavy burdens, and to let the oppressed go free, and that ye break every yoke?

7 *Is it* not to deal thy bread to the hungry, and that thou bring the poor that are cast out to thy house? when thou seest the naked, that thou cover him; and that thou hide not thyself from thine own flesh?

8 Then shall thy light break forth as the morning, and thine health shall spring forth speedily: and thy righteousness shall go before thee; the glory of the LORD shall be thy rereward.

9 Then shalt thou call, and the LORD shall answer; thou shalt cry, and he shall say, Here I *am.* If thou take away from the midst of thee the yoke, the putting forth of the finger, and speaking vanity;

10 And *if* thou draw out thy soul to the hungry, and satisfy the afflicted soul; then shall thy light rise in obscurity, and thy darkness *be* as the noonday:

11 And the LORD shall guide thee continually, and satisfy thy soul in drought, and make fat thy bones: and thou shalt be like a watered garden, and like a spring of water, whose waters fail not.

12 And *they that shall be* of thee shall build the old waste places: thou shalt raise up the foundations of many generations; and thou shalt be called, The repairer of the breach, The restorer of paths to dwell in.

13 If thou turn away thy foot from the sabbath, *from* doing thy pleasure on my holy day; and call the sabbath a delight, the holy of the LORD, honorable; and shalt honor him, not doing thine own ways, nor finding thine own pleasure, not speaking *thine own* words:

14 Then shalt thou delight thyself in the LORD; and I will cause thee to ride upon the high places of the earth, and feed thee with the heritage of Jacob thy father: for the mouth of the LORD hath spoken *it.*

Do you possess the strength to show compassion?

I tremble for my country when I reflect that God is just.

—Thomas Jefferson

There are many men and women who live in America (though it is a misuse of language to call them Americans) whose idea of liberty is to do precisely what they please, without reference to the health, comfort, peace, or even life of others; who translate the noble word liberty, with all its implications of self-restraint and self-sacrifice, into the anarchy of lawless self-assertion. By liberty they mean an unlimited opportunity of being selfish, discourteous, and disagreeable; by freedom they mean a chance to make life harder for their neighbors. They constitute an unresolved residuum of barbarism in a civilized society, and they make popular government unpopular with all who care enough for the people to be anxious for their morals or their manners.

—Lyman Abbott

War, being a consequence of the disregard of God, is not inevitable if man will turn to Him in repentance and obey His law. There is, then, no irresistible tide that is carrying man to destruction. Nothing is impossible with God.

—Amsterdam Assembly

Ill fares the land, to hastening ills a prey, where wealth accumulates, and men decay.

—Oliver Goldsmith

All that is necessary for the triumph of evil is that good men do nothing.

—Edmund Burke

A man protesting against error is on the way toward uniting himself with all men that believe in the truth

—Thomas Carlyle

Isaiah

1 Behold, the Lord's hand is not shortened, that it cannot save; neither his ear heavy, that it cannot hear:

2 But your iniquities have separated between you and your God, and your sins have hid *his* face from you, that he will not hear.

3 For your hands are defiled with blood, and your fingers with iniquity; your lips have spoken lies, your tongue hath muttered perverseness.

4 None calleth for justice, or *any* pleadeth for truth: they trust in vanity, and speak lies; they conceive mischief, and bring forth iniquity.

9 Therefore is judgment far from us, neither doth justice overtake us: we wait for light, but behold obscurity; for brightness, *but* we walk in darkness.

12 For our transgressions are multiplied before thee, and our sins testify against us: for our transgressions *are* with us; and *as for* our iniquities, we know them;

13 In transgressing and lying against the Lord, and departing away from our God, speaking oppression and revolt, conceiving and uttering from the heart words of falsehood.

14 And judgment is turned away backward, and justice standeth afar off; for truth is fallen in the street, and equity cannot enter.

15 Yea, truth faileth; and he *that* departeth from evil maketh himself a prey: and the Lord saw *it,* and it displeased him that *there was* no judgment.

16 And he saw that *there was* no man, and wondered that *there was* no intercessor: therefore his arm brought salvation unto him; and his righteousness, it sustained him.

17 For he put on righteousness as a breastplate, and a helmet of salvation upon his head; and he put on the garments of vengeance *for* clothing, and was clad with zeal as a cloak.

18 According to *their* deeds, accordingly he will repay, fury to his adversaries, recompense to his enemies; to the islands he will repay recompense.

19 So shall they fear the name of the Lord from the west, and his glory from the rising of the sun. When the enemy shall come in like a flood, the Spirit of the Lord shall lift up a standard against him.

20 And the Redeemer shall come to Zion, and unto them that turn from transgression in Jacob, saith the Lord.

21 As for me, this *is* my covenant with them, saith the Lord; My Spirit that *is* upon thee, and my words which I have put in thy mouth, shall not depart out of thy mouth, nor out of the mouth of thy seed, nor out of the mouth of thy seed's seed, saith the Lord, from henceforth and for ever.

The root of social evil is personal sin.

There are practical atheists who believe that they believe in God . . . but who in reality deny His existence by each one of their deeds.

—Jacques Maritain

God will estimate success one day.

—Robert Browning

Julia Ward Howe once wrote a U. S. Senator and solicited interest in a particular individual. The Senator wrote back: "I am so interested in the future of the race that I have no time for individuals." Mrs. Howe sent him a brief reply: "When God was last heard from, He had not reached that stage."

He who wins honor through his neighbor's shame will never reach paradise.

—Unknown

I am amused to see from my window here how busily man has divided and staked off his domain. God must smile at his puny fences running hither and thither everywhere over the land.

—Henry David Thoreau

He that turneth from the road to rescue another, turneth toward his goal; he shall arrive by the footpath of mercy; God will be his guide.

—Henry Van Dyke

Man should not consider his outward possessions as his own, but as common to all, so as to share them without hesitation when others are in need.

—Thomas Aquinas

10 He that is faithful in that which is least is faithful also in much: and he that is unjust in the least is unjust also in much.

11 If therefore ye have not been faithful in the unrighteous mammon, who will commit to your trust the true *riches*?

12 And if ye have not been faithful in that which is another man's, who shall give you that which is your own?

13 No servant can serve two masers: for either he will hate the one, and love the other; or else he will hold to the one, and despise the other. Ye cannot serve God and mammon.

14 And the Pharisees also, who were covetous, heard all these things: and they derided him.

15 And he said unto them, Ye are they which justify yourselves before men; but God knoweth your hearts: for that which is highly esteemed among men is abomination in the sight of God.

16 The law and the prophets *were* until John: since that time the kingdom of God is preached, and every man presseth into it.

17 And it is easier for heaven and earth to pass, than one tittle of the law to fail.

18 Whosoever putteth away his wife, and marrieth another, committeth adultery: and whosoever marrieth her that is put away from *her* husband committeth adultery.

19 There was a certain rich man, which was clothed in purple and fine linen, and fared sumptuously every day:

20 And there was a certain beggar named Lazarus, which was laid at his gate, full of sores,

21 And desiring to be fed with the crumbs which fell from the rich man's table: moreover the dogs came and licked his sores.

22 And it came to pass, that the beggar died, and was carried by the angels into Abraham's bosom: the rich man also died, and was buried;

23 And in hell he lifted up his eyes, being in torments, and seeth Abraham afar off, and Lazarus in his bosom.

24 And he cried and said, Father Abraham, have mercy on me, and send Lazarus, that he may dip the tip of his finger in water, and cool my tongue; for I am tormented in this flame.

25 But Abraham said, Son, remember that thou in thy lifetime receivedst thy good things, and likewise Lazarus evil things: but now he is comforted, and thou art tormented.

Can you be trusted?

No revolution that has ever taken place in society can be compared to that which has been produced by the words of Jesus Christ.

—Mark Hopkins

Try all the ways to peace and welfare you can think of, and you will find that there is no way that brings you to it except the way of Jesus.

—Matthew Arnold

It is a truth that stands out with startling distinctness on the pages of the New Testament, that God has no sons who are not servants.

—H. D. Ward

Faith is only worthy of the name when it erupts into action.

—Catherine Marshall

When you start a Bible movement, it means revolution—a quiet revolution against darkness and crime.

—Toyohiko Kagawa

The championship of social justice is almost the only way left nowadays to gain the crown of martrydom.

—Walter Rauschenbusch

Be ashamed to die until you have won some victory for humanity.

—Horace Mann

James

1 My brethren, have not the faith of our Lord Jesus Christ, *the* Lord of glory, with respect of persons.

5 Hearken, my beloved brethren, Hath not God chosen the poor of this world rich in faith, and heirs of the kingdom which he hath promised to them that love him?

6 But ye have despised the poor. Do not rich men oppress you, and draw you before the judgment seats?

7 Do not they blaspheme that worthy name by the which ye are called?

8 If ye fulfil the royal law according to the scripture, Thou shalt love thy neighbour as thyself, ye do well:

9 But if ye have respect to persons, ye commit sin, and are convinced of the law as transgressors.

10 For whosoever shall keep the whole law, and yet offend in one *point,* he is guilty of all.

11 For he that said, Do not commit adultery, said also, Do not kill. Now if thou commit no adultery, yet if thou kill, thou art become a transgressor of the law.

12 So speak ye, and so do, as they that shall be judged by the law of liberty.

13 For he shall have judgment without mercy, that hath shewed no mercy; and mercy rejoiceth against judgment.

14 What *doth it* profit, my brethren, though a man say he hath faith, and have not works? can faith save him?

15 If a brother or sister be naked, and destitute of daily food,

16 And one of you say unto them, Depart in peace, be *ye* warmed and filled; notwithstanding ye give them not those things which are needful to the body; what *doth it* profit?

17 Even so faith, if it hath not works, is dead, being alone.

18 Yea, a man may say, Thou hast faith, and I have works: shew me thy faith without thy works, and I will shew thee my faith by my works.

19 Thou believest that there is one God; thou doest well: the devils also believe, and tremble.

20 But wilt thou know, O vain man, that faith without works is dead?

21 Was not Abraham our father justified by works, when he had offered Isaac his son upon the altar?

22 Seest thou how faith wrought with his works, and by works was faith made perfect?

23 And the scripture was fulfilled which saith, Abraham believed God, and it was imputed unto him for righteousness: and he was called the Friend of God.

24 Ye see then how that by works a man is justified, and not by faith only.

26 For as the body without the spirit is dead, so faith without works is dead also.

Do you really love people?

Everybody thinks of changing humanity and nobody thinks of changing himself.

—Leo Tolstoy

We can never be the better for our religion if our neighbor is the worse for it.

—Unknown

Money never made a man happy yet, nor will it. There is nothing in its nature to produce happiness. The more a man has, the more he wants. Instead of filling a vacuum, it makes one. If it satisfied one want, it doubles and trebles that want another way. That was a true proverb of the wise man, rely on it: "Better is a little with the fear of the Lord, than great treasure and trouble therewith."

—Benjamin Franklin

Where money speaks the truth is silent.

—Unknown

We believe in man not merely as production units, but as the children of God. We believe that the purpose of our society is not primarily to assure "the safety of the State" but to safeguard human dignity and freedom of the individual.

—David Lilienthal

The beloved of the Almighty are the rich who have the humility of the poor, and the poor who have the magnanimity of the rich.

—Saadia ben Joseph

James

1 From whence *come* wars and fightings among you? *come they* not hence, *even* of your lusts that war in your members?

2 Ye lust, and have not: ye kill, and desire to have, and cannot obtain: ye fight and war, yet ye have not, because ye ask not.

3 Ye ask, and receive not, because ye ask amiss, that ye may consume *it* upon your lusts.

4 Ye adulterers and adulteresses, know ye not that the friendship of the world is enmity with God? whosoever therefore will be a friend of the world is the enemy of God.

5 Do ye think that the Scripture saith in vain, The spirit that dwelleth in us lusteth to envy?

6 But he giveth more grace. Wherefore he saith, God resisteth the proud, but giveth grace unto the humble.

7 Submit yourselves therefore to God. Resist the devil, and he will flee from you.

8 Draw nigh to God, and he will draw nigh to you. Cleanse *your* hands, *ye* sinners; and purify *your* hearts, *ye* double-minded.

9 Be afflicted, and mourn, and weep: let your laughter be turned to mourning, and *your* joy to heaviness.

10 Humble yourselves in the sight of the Lord, and he shall lift you up.

11 Speak not evil one of another, brethren. He that speaketh evil of *his* brother, and judgeth his brother, speaketh evil of the law, and judgeth the law: but if thou judge the law, thou art not a doer of the law, but a judge.

12 There is one lawgiver, who is able to save and to destroy: who art thou that judgest another?

13 Go to now, ye that say, Today or tomorrow we will go into such a city, and continue there a year, and buy and sell, and get gain:

14 Whereas ye know not what *shall be* on the morrow. For what *is* your life? It is even a vapor, that appeareth for a little time, and then vanisheth away.

15 For that ye *ought* to say, If the Lord will, we shall live, and do this, or that.

16 But now ye rejoice in your boastings: all such rejoicing is evil.

17 Therefore to him that knoweth to do good, and doeth *it* not, to him it is sin.

Humility before God eliminates strife among men.

Reflections

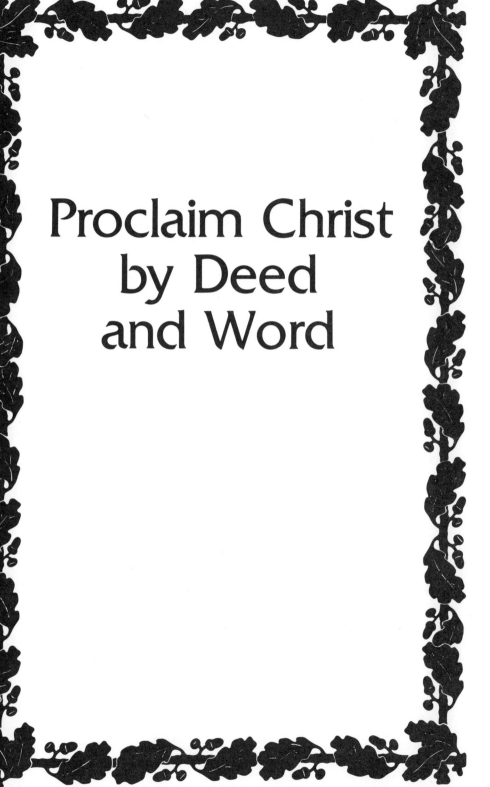

Proclaim Christ
by Deed
and Word

I will get ready and then perhaps my chance will come.

—Abraham Lincoln

It is not the critic who counts, not the man who points out how the strong man stumbled or where the doer of deeds could have done better. The credit belongs to the man who is actually in the arena; whose face is marred by dust and sweat and blood; who strives valiantly; who errs and comes short again and again; who knows the great enthusiasms, the great devotions, and spends himself in a worthy cause; who at the best knows in the end the triumph of high achievement and who at the worst, if he fails, at least fails while daring greatly; so that his place shall never be with those cold and timid souls who know neither victory nor defeat.

—Theodore Roosevelt

If I were not a follower of Christ, I think I should go mad, but my faith in God holds me to the belief that He is in some way working out His own plans through human perversities and mistakes.

—Woodrow Wilson

The greater thing in this world is not so much where we stand, as in what direction we are going.

—Oliver Wendell Holmes

It was for the love of the truths of this great and good Book that our fathers abandoned their native shore for the wilderness.

—Zachary Taylor

There is no man that hath left house, or parents, or brethren, or wife, or children, for the kingdom of God's sake, Who shall not receive manifold more in this present time, and in the world to come life everlasting.

—Luke 18:29,30

Genesis

1 Now the LORD had said unto Abram, Get thee out of thy country, and from thy kindred, and from thy father's house, unto a land that I will show thee:

2 And I will make of thee a great nation, and I will bless thee, and make thy name great; and thou shalt be a blessing:

3 And I will bless them that bless thee, and curse him that curseth thee: and in thee shall all families of the earth be blessed.

4 So Abram departed, as the LORD had spoken unto him; and Lot went with him: and Abraham *was* seventy and five years old when he departed out of Haran.

5 And Abram took Sarai his wife, and Lot his brother's son, and all their substance that they had gathered, and the souls that they had gotten in Haran; and they went forth to go into the land of Canaan; and into the land of Canaan they came.

6 And Abram passed through the land unto the place of Sichem, unto the plain of Moreh. And the Canaanite *was* then in the land.

7 And the LORD appeared unto Abram, and said, Unto thy seed will I give this land: and there builded he an altar unto the LORD, who appeared unto him.

8 And he removed from thence unto a mountain on the east of Bethel, and pitched his tent, *having* Bethel on the west, and Haion the east: and there he builded an altar unto the LORD, and called upon the name of the LORD.

9 And Abram journeyed, going on still toward the south.

CHAPTER 17

1 And when Abram was ninety years old and nine, the LORD appeared to Abram, and said unto him, I *am* the Almighty God; walk before me, and be thou perfect.

2 And I will make my covenant between me and thee, and will multiply thee exceedingly.

3 And Abram fell on his face: and God talked with him, saying.

4 As for me, behold, my covenant *is* with thee, and thou shalt be a father of many nations.

5 Neither shall thy name any more be called Abram, but thy name shall be Abraham; for a father of many nations have I made thee.

6 And I will make thee exceeding fruitful, and I will make nations of thee, and kings shall come out of thee.

7 And I will establish my covenant between me and thee and thy seed after thee in their generations, for an everlasting covenant, to be a God unto thee and to thy seed after thee.

8 And I will give unto thee, and to thy seed after thee, the land wherein thou art a stranger, all the land of Canaan, for an everlasting possession; and I will be their God.

Abraham believed God and went where God sent him.

The "great commitment" is so much easier than the ordinary one—and can all too easily shut our hearts to the latter. But without the humility and warmth which you have to develop in your relations to the few, with whom you are personally involved, you will never be able to do anything for the many.

—*Dag Hammarskjold*

The only significance of life consists in helping to establish the kingdom of God; and this can be done only by means of the acknowledgment and profession of the truth by each one of us.

—*Leo Tolstoy*

You give but little when you give of your possessions. It is when you give of yourself that you truly give.

—*Kahil Gibran*

If a man love the labor of any trade, apart from any question of success or fame, the gods have called him.

—*Robert Louis Stevenson*

Give us clear vision that we may know where to stand and what to stand for, because unless we stand for something, we shall fall for anything.

—*Peter Marshall*

O Lord, help us not to despise or oppose what we do not understand.

—*William Penn*

Vision is of God. A vision comes in advance of any task well done.

—*Katherine Logan*

1 Samuel

2 And it came to pass at that time, when Eli *was* laid down in his place, and his eyes began to wax dim, *that* he could not see;

3 And ere the lamp of God went out in the temple of the LORD, where the ark of God *was*, and Samuel was laid down *to sleep;*

4 That the LORD called Samuel: and he answered, Here *am* I.

5 And he ran unto Eli, and said, Here *am* I; for thou calledst me. And he said, I called not; lie down again. And he went and lay down.

6 And the LORD called yet again, Samuel. And Samuel arose and went to Eli, and said, Here *am* I; for thou didst call me. And he answered, I called not, my son; lie down again.

7 Now Samuel did not yet know the LORD, neither was the word of the LORD yet revealed unto him.

8 And the LORD called Samuel again the third time. And he arose and went to Eli, and said, Here *am* I; for thou didst call me. And Eli perceived that the LORD had called the child.

9 Therefore Eli said unto Samuel, Go, lie down: and it shall be, if he call thee, that thou shalt say, Speak, LORD; for thy servant heareth. So Samuel went and lay down in his place.

10 And the LORD came, and stood, and called as at other times, Samuel, Samuel. Then Samuel answered, Speak; for thy servant heareth.

11 And the LORD said to Samuel, Behold, I will do a thing in Israel, at which both the ears of every one that heareth it shall tingle.

12 In that day I will perform against Eli all *things* which I have spoken concerning his house: when I begin, I will also make an end.

13 For I have told him that I will judge his house for ever for the iniquity which he knoweth; because his sons made themselves vile, and he restrained them not.

14 And therefore I have sworn unto the house of Eli, that the iniquity of Eli's house shall not be purged with sacrifice nor offering for ever.

15 And Samuel lay until the morning, and opened the doors of the house of the LORD. And Samuel feared to show Eli the vision.

16 Then Eli called Samuel, and said, Samuel, my son. And he answered, Here *am* I.

17 And he said, What *is* the thing that *the* LORD hath said unto thee? I pray thee hide *it* not from me: God do so to thee, and more also, if thou hide *any* thing from me of all the things that he said unto thee.

18 And Samuel told him every whit, and hid nothing from him. And he said, It *is* the LORD: let him do what seemeth him good.

The only thing you should fear is ignoring the will of God.

If I were God, this world of sin and suffering would break my heart.

—Goethe

There is nothing so fatal to character as half-finished tasks.

—David Lloyd George

Who falls for love of God shall rise a star.

—Ben Jonson

The ultimate dedication is to truth—truth in every sense of the term, but especially truth as the fullness of being. Let every leader then examine himself as to the object of his dedication. . . . To the extent the dedication is to other than or less than the truth, the courage of the most courageous leader will gradually relent and wither away. The sense of untruth will eat at his heart and he will start giving in. The truth is that only the truth is worth living for, and he will display infinite courage who conceives his life a flame consuming itself at the altar of the truth.

—Charles Habib Malik

God offers to every mind its choice between truth and repose. Take which you please—you can never have both.

—Ralph Waldo Emerson

I have yet many things to say unto you, but ye cannot bear them now. . . . When . . . the Spirit of truth, is come, he will guide you into all truth. . . .

—John 16:12,13

Ezekiel

1 Again the word of the LORD came unto me, saying,

2 Son of man, speak to the children of thy people, and say unto them, When I bring the sword upon a land, if the people of the land take a man of their coasts, and set him for their watchman:

3 If when he seeth the sword come upon the land, he blow the trumpet, and warn the people;

4 Then whosoever heareth the sound of the trumpet, and taketh not warning; if the sword come, and take him away, his blood shall be upon his own head.

6 But if the watchman see the sword come, and blow not the trumpet, and the people be not warned; if the sword come, and take *any* person from among them, he is taken away in his iniquity; but his blood will I require at the watchman's hand.

7 So thou, O son of man, I have set thee a watchman unto the house of Israel; therefore thou shalt hear the word at my mouth, and warn them from me.

8 When I say unto the wicked, O wicked *man,* thou shalt surely die; if thou dost not speak to warn the wicked from his way, that wicked *man* shall die in his iniquity; but his blood will I require at thine hand.

9 Nevertheless, if thou warn the wicked of his way to turn from it; if he do not turn from his way, he shall die in his iniquity; but thou hast delivered thy soul.

10 Therefore, O thou son of man, speak unto the house of Israel; Thus ye speak, saying, If our transgressions and our sins *be* upon us, and we pine away in them, how should we then live?

11 Say unto them, *As* I live, saith the Lord GOD, I have no pleasure in the death of the wicked; but that the wicked turn from his way and live: turn ye, turn ye from your evil ways; for why will ye die, O house of Israel?

12 Therefore, thou son of man, say unto the children of thy people, The righteousness of the righteous shall not deliver him in the day of his transgression: as for the wickedness of the wicked, he shall not fall thereby in the day that he turneth from his wickedness; neither shall the righteous be able to live for his *righteousness* in the day that he sinneth.

17 Yet the children of thy people say, The way of the Lord is not equal: but as for them, their way is not equal.

18 When the righteous turneth from his righteousness, and committeth iniquity, he shall even die thereby.

19 But if the wicked turn from his wickedness, and do that which is lawful and right, he shall live thereby.

Has God ever commanded you to speak for Him?

The world has many religions; it has but one gospel.

—*George Owen*

I look upon the world as my parish.

—*John Wesley*

I have never heard anything about the resolutions of the apostles, but a good deal about the Acts of the apostles.

—*Horace Mann*

God hangs the greatest weights upon the smallest wires.

—*Francis Bacon*

The basic difference between physical and spiritual power is that men use physical power but spiritual power uses men.

—*Justin Wroe Nixon*

The great need of the world today is the spiritual power necessary for the overthrow of evil, for the establishment of righteousness, and for the ushering in of the era of perpetual peace; and that spiritual power begins in the surrender of the individual to God. It commences with obedience to the first commandment.

—*William Jennings Bryan*

It is not the business of a follower of Christ to provide an organization for the world, but to infuse the Spirit of Christ into the organizations of the world.

—*Unknown*

Matthew

1 In the end of the sabbath, as it began to dawn toward the first *day* of the week, came Mary Magdalene and the other Mary to see the sepulchre.

2 And, behold, there was a great earthquake: for the angel of the Lord descended from heaven, and came and rolled back the stone from the door, and sat upon it.

3 His countenance was like lightning, and his raiment white as snow:

4 And for fear of him the keepers did shake, and became as dead *men*.

5 And the angel answered and said unto the women, Fear not ye: for I know that ye seek Jesus, which was crucified.

6 He is not here: for he is risen, as he said. Come, see the place where the Lord lay.

7 And go quickly, and tell his disciples that he is risen from the dead; and, behold, he goeth before you into Galilee; there shall ye see him: lo, I have told you.

8 And they departed quickly from the sepulchre with fear and great joy; and did run to bring his disciples word.

9 And as they went to tell his disciples, behold, Jesus met them, saying, All hail. And they came and held him by the feet, and worshipped him.

10 Then said Jesus unto them, Be not afraid: go tell my brethren that they go into Galilee, and there shall they see me.

11 Now when they were going, behold, some of the watch came into the city, and showed unto the chief priests all the things that were done.

12 And when they were assembled with the elders, and had taken counsel, they gave large money unto the soldiers,

13 Saying, Say ye, His disciples came by night, and stole him *away* while we slept.

14 And if this come to the governor's ears, we will persuade him, and secure you.

15 So they took the money, and did as they were taught: and this saying is commonly reported among the Jews until this day.

16 Then the eleven disciples went away into Galilee, into a mountain where Jesus had appointed them.

17 And when they saw him, they worshipped him: but some doubted.

18 And Jesus came and spake unto them, saying, All power is given unto me in heaven and in earth.

19 Go ye therefore, and teach all nations, baptizing them in the name of the Father, and of the Son, and of the Holy Ghost:

20 Teaching them to observe all things whatsoever I have commanded you: and, lo, I am with you alway, *even* unto the end of the world. Amen.

The authority and power is Christ's and He wants to exhibit it through you.

In simple trust like theirs who heard
Beside the Syrian sea
The gracious calling of the Lord,
Let us, like them, without a word
Rise up and follow Thee.

—John Greenleaf Whittier

Following Christ can be condensed into four words: admit, submit, commit, and transmit.

—Samuel Wilberforce

With God, go over the sea—without Him, not over the threshold.

—Unknown

Though we live in a reading age and in a reading community, yet the preaching of the gospel is the form in which human agency has been and still is most efficaciously employed for the spiritual improvement of men.

—Daniel Webster

Day by day, it becomes more apparent that problems would be impossible of solutions and temptations impossible of resistance, without the divine help which is offered us in abundance. But each day it becomes more apparent, also, that God expects of us not only prayer, but good works as well.

—Richard B. Ogilvie

The sages and heroes of history are receding from us, and history contracts the record of their deeds into a narrower and narrower page. But time has no power over the name and deeds and words of Jesus Christ.

—William Ellery Channing

Luke

57 And it came to pass, that, as they went in the way, a certain *man* said unto him, Lord, I will follow thee whithersoever thou goest.

58 And Jesus said unto him, Foxes have holes, and birds of the air *have* nests; but the Son of man hath not where to lay *his* head.

59 And he said unto another, Follow me. But he said, Lord, suffer me first to go and bury my father.

60 Jesus said unto him, Let the dead bury their dead; but go thou and preach the kingdom of God.

61 And another also said, Lord, I will follow thee; but let me first go bid them farewell, which are at home at my house.

62 And Jesus said unto him, No man, having put his hand to the plow, and looking back, is fit for the kingdom of God.

CHAPTER 10

1 After these things the Lord appointed other seventy also, and sent them two and two before his face into every city and place, whither he himself would come.

2 Therefore said he unto them, The harvest truly *is* great, but the laborers *are* few: pray ye therefore the Lord of the harvest, that he would send forth laborers into his harvest.

3 Go your ways: behold, I send you forth as lambs among wolves.

4 Carry neither purse, nor scrip, nor shoes: salute no man by the way.

5 And into whatsoever house ye enter, first say, Peace *be* to this house.

6 And if the son of peace be there, your peace shall rest upon it: if not, it shall turn to you again.

7 And in the same house remain, eating and drinking such things as they give: for the laborer is worthy of his hire. Go not from house to house.

8 And into whatsoever city ye enter, and they receive you, eat such things as are set before you:

9 And heal the sick that are therein, and say unto them, The kingdom of God is come nigh unto you.

10 But into whatsoever city ye enter, and they receive you not, go your ways out into the streets of the same, and say,

11 Even the very dust of your city, which cleaveth on us, we do wipe off against you: notwithstanding, be ye sure of this, that the kingdom of God is come nigh unto you.

12 But I say unto you, that it shall be more tolerable in that day for Sodom, than for that city.

16 He that heareth you heareth me; and he that despiseth you despiseth me; and he that despiseth me despiseth him that sent me.

Follow Jesus Christ.

There is no mistake so bad . . . as the greatest mistake of saying nothing for Christ.

> —*Henry Clay Trumbull*

I look upon foreign missionaries as the scaffolding around a rising building. The sooner it can be dispensed with, the better; or rather, the sooner it can be transferred to the other places, to serve the same temporary use, the better.

> —*Hudson Taylor*

Perish discretion where it interferes with duty.

> —*H. More*

The love of God is the ultimate reality, the deepest and strongest force in the universe; and it is revealed to the man who resolutely girds himself to the conflict.

> —*David Smith*

They are the true disciples of Christ, not who know most, but who love most.

> —*Frederich Spanheim the Elder*

God evidently does not intend us all to be rich, or powerful or great, but He does intend us all to be friends.

> —*Ralph Waldo Emerson*

By friendship you mean the greatest love, the greatest usefulness, the most open communication, the noblest sufferings, the severest truth, the heartiest counsel, and the greatest union of minds of which brave men and women are capable.

> —*Jeremy Taylor*

John

1 I am the true vine and my Father is the husbandman.

4 Abide in me, and I in you. As the branch cannot bear fruit of itself, except it abide in the vine; no more can ye, except ye abide in me.

5 I am the vine, ye *are* the branches. He that abideth in me, and I in him, the same bringeth forth much fruit; for without me ye can do nothing.

6 If a man abide not in me, he is cast forth as a branch, and is withered; and men gather them, and cast *them* into the fire, and they are burned.

7 If ye abide in me, and my words abide in you, ye shall ask what ye will, and it shall be done unto you.

8 Herein is my Father glorified, that ye bear much fruit; so shall ye be my disciples.

9 As the Father hath loved me, so have I loved you: continue ye in my love.

10 If ye keep my commandments, ye shall abide in my love; even as I have kept my Father's commandments, and abide in his love.

13 Greater love hath no man than this, that a man lay down his life for his friends.

14 Ye are my friends, if ye do whatsoever I command you.

15 Henceforth I call you not servants; for the servant knoweth not what his lord doeth: but I have called you friends; for all things that I have heard of my Father I have made known unto you.

16 Ye have not chosen me, but I have chosen you, and ordained you, that ye should go and bring forth fruit, and *that* your fruit should remain; that whatsoever ye shall ask of the Father in my name, he may give it you.

17 These things I command you, that ye love one another.

18 If the world hate you, ye know that it hated me before *it hated* you.

19 If ye were of the world, the world would love his own; but because ye are not of the world, but I have chosen you out of the world, therefore the world hateth you.

20 Remember the word that I said unto you, The servant is not greater than his lord. If they have persecuted me, they will also persecute you; if they have kept my saying, they will keep yours also.

21 But all these things will they do unto you for my name's sake, because they know not him that sent me.

22 If I had not come and spoken unto them, they had not had sin; but now they have no cloak for their sin.

26 But when the Comforter is come, whom I will send unto you from the Father, *even* the Spirit of truth, which proceedeth from the Father, he shall testify of me:

27 And ye also shall bear witness, because ye have been with me from the beginning.

We are called to share a task with a Friend.

Wherefore God also hath highly exalted him, and given him a name which is above every name: That at the name of Jesus every knee should bow . . . And that every tongue should confess that Jesus Christ is Lord, to the glory of God the Father.

—Philippians 2:9-11

In his life Christ is an example showing us how to live; in His death, He is a sacrifice satisfying for our sins; in His resurrection, a conqueror; in His ascension, a king; in His intercession, a high priest.

—Martin Luther

Behold, I stand at the door and knock: if any man hear my voice, and open the door, I will come in to him, and will sup with him, and he with me.

—Revelation 3:20

Jesus Christ, the condescension of divinity and the exaltation of humanity.

—Phillip Brooks

Let every kindred, every tribe
    On this terrestrial ball,
To Him all majesty ascribe
    And crown Him Lord of all.

—Edward Perronet

The tongue blessing God without the heart is but a tinkling cymbal; the heart blessing God without the tongue is sweet but still music; both in concert make the harmony which fills and delights heaven and earth.

—R. Venning

A child of God should be a visible beatitude for joy and happiness, and a living doxology for gratitude and adoration.

—Charles Spurgeon

Romans

1 Brethren, my heart's desire and prayer to God for Israel is, that they might be saved.

2 For I bear them record that they have a zeal of God, but not according to knowledge.

3 For they, being ignorant of God's righteousness, and going about to establish their own righteousness, have not submitted themselves unto the righteousness of God.

4 For Christ *is* the end of the law for righteousness to every one that believeth.

5 For Moses describeth the righteousness which is of the law, That the man which doeth those things shall live by them.

6 But the righteousness which is of faith speaketh on this wise, Say not in thine heart, Who shall ascend into heaven? (that is, to bring Christ down *from above:*)

7 Or, Who shall descend into the deep? (that is, to bring up Christ again from the dead.)

8 But what saith it? The word is nigh thee, *even* in thy mouth, and in thy heart: that is, the word of faith, which we preach;

9 That if thou shalt confess with thy mouth the Lord Jesus, and shalt believe in thine heart that God hath raised him from the dead, thou shalt be saved.

10 For with the heart man believeth unto righteousness; and with the mouth confession is made unto salvation.

11 For the Scripture saith, Whosoever believeth on him shall not be ashamed.

12 For there is no difference between the Jew and the Greek: for the same Lord over all is rich unto all that call upon him.

13 For whosoever shall call upon the name of the Lord shall be saved.

14 How then shall they call on him in whom they have not believed? and how shall they believe in him of whom they have not heard? and how shall they hear without a preacher?

15 And how shall they preach, except they be sent? as it is written, How beautiful are the feet of them that preach the gospel of peace, and bring glad tidings of good things!

16 But they have not all obeyed the gospel. For Esaias saith, Lord, who hath believed our report?

17 So then faith *cometh* by hearing, and hearing by the word of God.

18 But I say, Have they not heard? Yes verily, their sound went into all the earth, and their words unto the ends of the world.

19 But I say, Did not Israel know? First Moses saith, I will provoke you to jealousy by *them that are* no people, *and* by a foolish nation I will anger you.

21 But to Israel he saith, All day long I have stretched forth my hands unto a disobedient and gainsaying people.

Confess with your mouth—believe in your heart.

Tho' Christ a thousand times in Bethlehem be born,
If He's not born in thee, thy soul is still forlorn.

—Johannes Scheffler

So . . . comes a human voice,
Saying: "O heart I made a heart beats here;
Face my hands fashioned see it in myself;
Thou hast no strength, nor mayst conceive of mine;
But love I gave thee, with myself to love,
And thou must love me who have died for thee."

—Robert Browning

What I want is, not to possess a mere belief, but to be possessed by Christ and
His commandments.

—Unknown

The satisfaction of Christ is to free us from misery; the merit of Christ is to
purchase happiness for us.

—Jonathan Edwards

It is natural to be religious; it is supernatural to follow Christ.

—Unknown

Batter my heart, three personed God; for you
As yet but knock, breathe, shine, and seek to mend;
That I may rise, and stand, o'erthrow me, and bend
Your force to break, blow, burn, and make me new.

—John Donne

If we can seek, find, and evoke the Spirit and teaching of Christ in men in
their daily lives, we might more nearly approximate the practical genius of
that first-century faith, and in Christ Himself discover for ourselves the
transforming power of God.

—Henry H. Fowler

II Corinthians

1 For we know that, if our earthly house of *this* tabernacle were dissolved, we have a building of God, a house not made with hands, eternal in the heavens.

4 For we that are in *this* tabernacle do groan, being burdened: not for that we would be unclothed, but clothed upon, that morality might be swallowed up of life.

5 Now he that hath wrought us for the selfsame thing *is* God, who also hath given unto us the earnest of the Spirit.

6 Therefore *we are* always confident, knowing that, whilst we are at home in the body, we are absent from the Lord:

7 (For we walk by faith, not by sight:)

8 We are confident, I *say,* and willing rather to be absent from the body, and to be present with the Lord.

9 Wherefore we labour, that, whether present or absent, we may be accepted of him.

10 For we must all appear before the judgment seat of Christ; that every one may receive the things *done* in his *body,* according to that he hath done, whether *it be* good or bad.

11 Knowing therefore the terror of the Lord, we persuade men; but we are made manifest unto God; and I trust also are made manifest in your consciences.

14 For the love of Christ constraineth us; because we thus judge, that if one died for all, then were all dead:

15 And *that* he died for all, that they which live should not henceforth live unto themselves, but unto him which died for them, and rose again.

16 Wherefore henceforth know we no man after the flesh: yea, though we have known Christ after the flesh, yet now henceforth know we *him* no more.

17 Therefore if any man *be* in Christ, *he is* a new creature: old things are passed away; behold, all things are become new.

18 And all things *are* of God, who hath reconciled us to himself by Jesus Christ, and hath given to us the ministry of reconciliation;

19 To wit, that God was in Christ, reconciling the world unto himself, not imputing their trespasses unto them; and hath committed unto us the word of reconciliation.

20 Now then we are ambassadors for Christ, as though God did beseech *you* by us: we pray *you* in Christ's stead, be ye reconciled to God.

21 For he hath made him *to be* sin for us, who knew no sin; that we might be made the righteousness of God in him.

Become a new person in Christ.

Reflections

A Leadership
Led by God

We cannot decide whether or not we will live or die; we can only decide what we will die for.

—Bob Pierce

I beseech you therefore, brethren, by the mercies of God, that ye present your bodies a living sacrifice, holy, acceptable unto God, which is your reasonable service.

—Romans 12:1.

It is not to a life of ease and mediocrity that Christ has called us, but to the disciple-like, Christ-empowered life demonstrated by men of former generations. Only by such lives can we hope to meet the urgency of this hour.

—Mark O. Hatfield

Blessed are ye, when men shall revile you, and persecute you, and shall say all manner of evil against you falsely, for my sake. Rejoice, and be exceeding glad: for great is your reward in heaven: for so persecuted they the prophets which were before you.

—Matthew 5:11,12

Men may misjudge thy aim,
Think they have cause to blame,
Say thou art wrong:
Keep on the quiet way,
Christ is the Judge, not they,
Fear not, be strong.

—Unknown

I would a great deal rather lose in a cause that I know some day will triumph than triumph in a cause that I know will some day lose.

—Woodrow Wilson

Genesis

5 And God saw that the wickedness of man *was* great in the earth, and *that* every imagination of the thoughts of his heart *was* only evil continually.

6 And it repented the LORD that he had made man on the earth, and it grieved him at his heart.

7 And the LORD said, I will destroy man whom I have created from the face of the earth; both man, and beast, and the creeping thing, and the fowls of the air; for it repenteth me that I have made them.

8 But Noah found grace in the eyes of the LORD.

9 These *are* the generations of Noah: Noah was a just man *and* perfect in his generations, *and* Noah walked with God.

10 And Noah begat three sons, Shem, Ham, and Japheth.

11 The earth also was corrupt before God; and the earth was filled with violence.

12 And God looked upon the earth, and, behold, it was corrupt; for all flesh had corrupted his way upon the earth.

13 And God said unto Noah, The end of all flesh is come before me; for the earth is filled with violence through them; and, behold, I will destroy them with the earth.

14 Make thee an ark of gopher wood; rooms shalt thou make in the ark, and shalt pitch it within and without with pitch.

15 And this *is the fashion* which thou shalt make it *of:* The length of the ark *shall be* three hundred cubits, the breadth of it fifty cubits, and the height of it thirty cubits.

16 A window shalt thou make to the ark, and in a cubit shalt thou finish it above; and the door of the ark shalt thou set in the side thereof; *with* lower, second, and third *stories* shalt thou make it.

17 And, behold, I, even I, do bring a flood of waters upon the earth, to destroy all flesh, wherein *is* the breath of life, from under heaven; *and* every thing that *is* in the earth shall die.

18 But with thee will I establish my covenant; and thou shalt come into the ark, thou, and thy sons, and thy wife, and thy sons' wives with thee.

19 And of every living thing of all flesh, two of every sort shalt thou bring into the ark, to keep *them* alive with thee; they shall be male and female.

20 Of fowls after their kind, and of cattle after their kind, of every creeping thing of the earth after his kind; two of every *sort* shall come unto thee, to keep *them* alive.

21 And take thou unto thee of all food that is eaten, and thou shalt gather *it* to thee; and it shall be for food for thee, and for them.

22 Thus did Noah; according to all that God commanded him, so did he.

Are you willing to be ridiculed for a good cause?

The prosperity of a country depends, not on the abundance of its revenues, nor on the strength of its fortifications, nor on the beauty of its public buildings, but it consists in the number of its men of enlightenment and character.

—Martin Luther

The best executive is the one who has sense enough to pick good men to do what he wants done, and self-restraint enough to keep from meddling with them while they do it.

—Theodore Roosevelt

God governs the world, and we have only to do our duty wisely, and leave the issue to Him.

—John Jay

Destiny waits in the hand of God, not in the hands of statesmen.

—T. S. Eliot

Nations would be terrified if they knew by what small men they were ruled.

—Charles Talleyrand

God give us men. A time like this demands strong minds, great hearts, true faith, and ready hands! Men whom the lust of office does not kill, men whom the spoils of office cannot buy, men who possess opinions and a will, men who love honor, men who cannot lie.

—J. G. Holland

No man rules safely but he that is willingly ruled.

—Thomas à Kempis

Exodus

13 And it came to pass on the morrow, that Moses sat to judge the people: and the people stood by Moses from the morning unto the evening.

14 And when Moses' father-in-law saw all that he did to the people, he said, What *is* this thing that thou doest to the people? Why sittest thou thyself alone, and all people stand by thee from morning unto even?

15 And Moses said unto his father-in-law, Because the people come unto me to inquire of God:

16 When they have a matter, they come unto me; and I judge between one and another, and I do make *them* know the statutes of God, and his laws.

17 And Moses' father-in-law said unto him, The thing that thou doest *is* not good.

18 Thou wilt surely wear away, both thou, and this people that *is* with thee: for this thing *is* too heavy for thee; thou art not able to perform it thyself alone.

19 Hearken now unto my voice, I will give thee counsel, and God shall be with thee: Be thou for the people to Godward, that thou mayest bring the causes unto God:

20 And thou shalt teach them ordinances and laws, and shalt show them the way wherein they must walk, and the work that they must do.

21 Moreover thou shalt provide out of all the people able men, such as fear God, men of truth, hating covetousness; and place *such* over them, *to be* rulers of thousands, *and* rulers of hundreds, rulers of fifties, and rulers of tens:

22 And let them judge the people at all seasons: and it shall be, *that* every great matter they shall bring unto thee, but every small matter they shall judge: so shall it be easier for thyself, and they shall bear *the burden* with thee.

23 If thou shalt do this thing, and God command thee *so*, then thou shalt be able to endure, and all this people shall also go to their place in peace.

24 So Moses hearkened to the voice of his father-in-law, and did all that he had said.

25 And Moses chose able men out of all Israel, and made them heads over the people, rulers of thousands, rulers of hundreds, rulers of fifties, and rulers of tens.

26 And they judged the people at all seasons: the hard causes they brought unto Moses, but every small matter they judged themselves.

Do you trust others to help?

To let oneself be bound by a duty from the moment you see it approaching is part of the integrity that alone justifies responsibility.

—Dag Hammarskjold

Leadership is the ability to generate, communicate, and maintain commonality of purpose.

—Unknown

Those who are greedy of praise prove that they are poor in merit.

—Plutarch

I had rather men should ask why no statue has been erected in my honor, than why one has.

—Marcus Cato

The best exercise for the heart is to reach down and pull other people up.

—Unknown

A leader is best
when people barely know he exists.
Not so good
when people obey and claim him.
Worse when they despise him.
But of a good leader
who talks little
when his work is done
his aims fulfilled
they will say:
"We did it ourselves."

—Lao-tse (565 B.C.)

Matthew

17 And Jesus going up to Jerusalem took the twelve disciples apart in the way, and said unto them,

18 Behold, we go up to Jerusalem; and the Son of man shall be betrayed unto the chief priests and unto the scribes, and they shall condemn him to death,

19 And shall deliver him to the Gentiles to mock, and to scourge, and to crucify *him:* and the third day he shall rise again.

20 Then came to him the mother of Zebedee's children with her sons, worshipping *him,* and desiring a certain thing of him.

21 And he said unto her, What wilt thou? She saith unto him, Grant that these my two sons may sit, the one on thy right hand, and the other on the left, in thy kingdom.

22 But Jesus answered and said, Ye know not what ye ask. Are ye able to drink of the cup that I shall drink of, and to be baptized with the baptism that I am baptized with? They say unto him, We are able.

23 And he saith unto them, Ye shall drink indeed of my cup, and be baptized with the baptism that I am baptized with: but to sit on my right hand, and on my left, is not mine to give, but *it shall be given to them* for whom it is prepared of my Father.

24 And when the ten heard *it,* they were moved with indignation against the two brethren.

25 But Jesus called *unto him,* and said, Ye know that the princes of the Gentiles exercise dominion over them, and they that are great exercise authority upon them.

26 But it shall not be so among you: but whosoever will be great among you, let him be your minister;

27 And whosoever will be chief among you, let him be your servant:

28 Even as the Son of man came not to be ministered unto, but to minister, and to give his life a ransom for many.

29 And as they departed from Jericho, a great multitude followed him.

30 And, behold, two blind men sitting by the wayside, when they heard that Jesus passed by, cried out, saying, Have mercy on us, O Lord, *thou* Son of David.

31 And the multitude rebuked them, because they should hold their peace: but they cried the more, saying, Have mercy on us, O Lord, *thou* Son of David.

32 And Jesus stood still, and called them, and said, What will ye that I shall do unto you?

33 They say unto him, Lord, that our eyes may be opened.

34 So Jesus had compassion *on them,* and touched their eyes: and immediately their eyes received sight, and they followed him.

Why not follow the example of Jesus Christ?

Try all the ways of peace and welfare you can think of, and you will find that there is no way that brings you to it except the way of Jesus. But this way does bring it to you.

—*Matthew Arnold*

I have read in Plato and Cicero sayings that are very wise and very beautiful; but I never read in either of them: "Come unto me all ye that labor and are heavy laden."

—*Augustine*

Feed on Christ, and then go and live your life, and it is Christ in you that lives your life, that helps the poor, that tells the truth, that fights the battle, and that wins the crown.

—*Phillips Brooks*

Jesus Christ is in the noblest and most perfect sense the realized ideal of humanity.

—*Johann Gottfried von Herder*

The final test of a leader is that he leaves behind him in other men the conviction and the will to carry on. . . . The genius of a good leader is to leave behind him a situation which common sense, without the grace of genius, can deal with successfully.

—*Walter Lippmann*

Lie down till the leaders have spoken—it may be fair words shall prevail.

—*Rudyard Kipling*

Matthew

12 And whosoever shall exalt himself shall be abased; and he that shall humble himself shall be exalted.

13 But woe unto you, scribes and Pharisees, hypocrites! for ye shut up the kingdom of heaven against men: for ye neither go in *yourselves,* neither suffer ye them that are entering to go in.

14 Woe unto you, scribes and Pharisees, hypocrites! for ye devour widows' houses, and for a pretense make long prayer: therefore ye shall receive the greater damnation.

15 Woe unto you, scribes and Pharisees, hypocrites! for ye compass sea and land to make one proselyte; and when he is made, ye make him twofold more the child of hell than yourselves.

16 Woe unto you, *ye* blind guides, which say, Whosoever shall swear by the temple, it is nothing; but whosoever shall swear by the gold of the temple, he is a debtor!

17 *Ye* fools and blind: for whether is greater, the gold, or the temple that sanctifieth the gold?

18 And, Whosoever shall swear by the altar, it is nothing; but whosoever sweareth by the gift that is upon it, he is guilty.

19 *Ye* fools and blind: for whether *is* greater, the gift, or the altar that sanctifieth the gift?

20 Whoso therefore shall swear by the altar, sweareth by it, and by all things thereon.

21 And whoso shall swear by the temple, sweareth by it, and by him that dwelleth therein.

22 And he that shall swear by heaven, sweareth by the throne of God, and by him that sitteth thereon.

23 Woe unto you, scribes and Pharisees, hypocrites! for ye pay tithe of mint and anise and cummin, and have omitted the weightier *matters* of the law, judgment, mercy, and faith: these ought ye to have done, and not to leave the other undone.

24 *Ye* blind guides, which strain at a gnat, and swallow a camel.

25 Woe unto you, scribes and Pharisees, hypocrites! for ye make clean the outside of the cup and of the platter, but within they are full of extortion and excess.

26 *Thou* blind Pharisee, cleanse first that *which is* within the cup and platter, that the outside of them may be clean also.

27 Woe unto you, scribes and Pharisees, hypocrites! for ye are like unto whited sepulchres, which indeed appear beautiful outward, but are within full of dead *men's* bones, and of all uncleanness.

28 Even so ye also outwardly appear righteous unto men, but within ye are full of hypocrisy and iniquity.

Don't be a blind leader—follow Jesus Christ.

Show me the kind of man you honor, and I will know what kind of man you are, for it shows me what your ideal of manhood is, and what kind of man you long to be.

—*Thomas Carlyle*

Example is the school of mankind, and they will learn at no other.

—*Edmund Burke*

The path of precept is long, that of example short and effectual.

—*Seneca*

Precepts may lead, but examples draw.

—*H. G. Bohn*

I have ever deemed it more honorable and more profitable, to set a good example than to follow a bad one.

—*Thomas Jefferson*

In our great pride at being the arsenal of democracy we must remember that we are also regarded as the arsenal of hope. Great leadership in such a righteous cause requires that a nation be humble—before God and its fellow men.

—*Omar N. Bradley*

And every one that was in distress, and every one that was in debt, and every one that was discontented, gathered themselves unto him; and he became a captain over them: and there were with him about four hundred men.

—*1 Samuel 22:2*

John

1 Now before the feast of the passover, when Jesus knew that his hour was come that he should depart out of this world unto the Father, having loved his own which were in the world, he loved them unto the end.

2 And supper being ended, the devil having now put into the heart of Judas Iscariot, Simon's *son,* to betray him;

3 Jesus knowing that the Father had given all things into his hands, and that he was come from God, and went to God;

4 He riseth from supper, and laid aside his garments; and took a towel, and girded himself.

5 After that he poureth water into a bason, and began to wash the disciples' feet, and to wipe *them* with the towel wherewith he was girded.

6 Then cometh he to Simon Peter: and Peter saith unto him, Lord, dost thou wash my feet?

7 Jesus answered and said unto him, What I do thou knowest not now; but thou shalt know hereafter.

8 Peter saith unto him, Thou shalt never wash my feet. Jesus answered him, If I wash thee not, thou hast no part with me.

9 Simon Peter saith unto him, Lord, not my feet only, but also *my* hands and *my* head.

10 Jesus saith to him, He that is washed needeth not save to wash *his* feet, but is clean every whit: and ye are clean, but not all.

11 For he knew who should betray him; therefore said he, Ye are not all clean.

12 So after he had washed their feet, and had taken his garments, and was set down again, he said unto them, Know ye what I have done to you?

13 Ye call me Master and Lord: and ye say well; for *so* I am.

14 If I then, *your* Lord and Master, have washed your feet; ye also ought to wash one another's feet.

15 For I have given you an example, that ye should do as I have done to you.

16 Verily, verily, I say unto you, The servant is not greater than his lord; neither he that is sent greater than he that sent him.

17 If ye know these things, happy are ye if ye do them.

18 I speak not of you all: I know whom I have chosen: but that the Scripture may be fulfilled, He that eateth bread with me hath lifted up his heel against me.

19 Now I tell you before it come, that, when it is come to pass, ye may believe that I am *he.*

20 Verily, verily, I say unto you, He that receiveth whomsoever I send receiveth me; and he that receiveth me receiveth him that sent me.

To lead is to serve; to serve you must have confidence in God.

The men who succeed best in public life are those who take the risk of standing by their own convictions.

—James A. Garfield

The man who is to take a high place before his fellows must take a low place before his God.

—Unknown

No one is dressed shabbier than he who uses his religion as a cloak.

—David Young

To sin by silence when they should protest makes cowards of men.

—Abraham Lincoln

Jesus astonishes and overpowers sensual people. They cannot unite Him to history or reconcile Him with themselves.

—Ralph Waldo Emerson

No man can follow Christ and go astray.

—Frederic W. Farrar

A determined soul will do more with a rusty monkey-wrench than a loafer will accomplish with all the tools in a machine shop.

—Rupert Hughes

Nobody will know what you mean by saying that "God is love" unless you act it as well.

—Lawrence Pearsall Jacks

1 Timothy

1 I exhort therefore, that, first of all, supplications, prayers, intercessions, *and* giving of thanks, be made for all men;

2 For kings, and *for* all that are in authority; that we may lead a quiet and peaceable life in all godliness and honesty.

3 For this *is* good and acceptable in the sight of God our Saviour;

4 Who will have all men to be saved, and to come unto the knowledge of the truth.

5 For *there is* one God, and one mediator between God and men, the man Christ Jesus;

6 Who gave himself a ransom for all, to be testified in due time.

7 Whereunto I am ordained a preacher, and an apostle, (I speak the truth in Christ, *and* lie not,) a teacher of the Gentiles in faith and verity.

8 I will therefore that men pray every where, lifting up holy hands, without wrath and doubting.

CHAPTER 3

1 This *is* a true saying, If a man desire the office of a bishop, he desireth a good work.

2 A bishop then must be blameless, the husband of one wife, vigilant, sober, of good behavior, given to hospitality, apt to teach;

3 Not given to wine, no striker, not greedy of filthy lucre; but patient, not a brawler, not covetous;

4 One that ruleth well his own house, having his children in subjection with all gravity;

5 (For if a man know not how to rule his own house, how shall he take care of the church of God?)

6 Not a novice, lest being lifted up with pride he fall into the condemnation of the devil.

7 Moreover he must have a good report of them which are without; lest he fall into reproach and the snare of the devil.

8 Likewise *must* the deacons *be* grave, not double-tongued, not given to much wine, not greedy of filthy lucre;

9 Holding the mystery of the faith in a pure conscience.

10 And let these also first be proved; then let them use the office of a deacon, being *found* blameless.

13 For they that have used the office of a deacon well purchase to themselves a good degree, the great boldness in the faith which is in Christ Jesus.

14 These things write I unto thee, hoping to come unto thee shortly:

15 But if I tarry long, that thou mayest know how thou oughtest to behave thyself in the house of God, which is the church of the living God, the pillar and ground of the truth.

16 And without controversy great is the mystery of godliness: God was manifest in the flesh, justified in the Spirit, seen of angels, preached unto the Gentiles, believed on in the world, received up into glory.

The leader's first responsibility is to be a fit example.

I think the key here is man must build relationships around the world, and trust, and love, and understanding. He can't just talk about this, but he must attempt to find concrete ways by which he makes this a reality. . . . If we have that kind of love and understanding then I think you will see a different world today.

—*John Staggers*

The men who are lifting the world upward and onward are those who encourage more than criticize.

—*Elizabeth Harrison*

He who sincerely praises God will soon discover within his soul an inclination to praise goodness in his fellow man.

—*Oliver G. Wilson*

One man working *with* you is worth a dozen men working *for* you.

—*Herman H. Kolliker*

No true and permanent fame can be founded except in the labors which promote the happiness of mankind.

—*Charles Sumner*

The best kind of leadership is that which produces fellowship.

—*Unknown*

The price of a bridge is often measured in the lives of its builders. For he who would build a bridge must be ready to pay for it with his life.

—*Pen Lyle Pittard*

Philemon

1 Paul, a prisoner of Jesus Christ, and Timothy *our* brother, unto Philemon our dearly beloved, and fellow labourer,

3 Grace to you, and peace, from God our Father and the Lord Jesus Christ.

4 I thank my God, making mention of thee always in my prayers,

5 Hearing of thy love and faith, which thou hast toward the Lord Jesus, and toward all saints;

6 That the communication of thy faith may become effectual by the acknowledging of every good thing which is in you in Christ Jesus.

7 For we have great joy and consolation in thy love, because the bowels of the saints are refreshed by thee, brother.

8 Wherefore, though I might be much bold in Christ to enjoin thee that which is convenient,

9 Yet for love's sake I rather beseech *thee,* being such a one as Paul the aged, and now also a prisoner of Jesus Christ.

10 I beseech thee for my son Onesimus, whom I have begotten in my bonds:

11 Which in time past was to thee unprofitable, but now profitable to thee and to me:

12 Whom I have sent again: thou therefore receive him, that is, mine own bowels:

13 Whom I would have retained with me, that in thy stead he might have ministered unto me in the bonds of the gospel:

14 But without thy mind would I do nothing; that thy benefit should not be as it were of necessity, but willingly.

15 For perhaps he therefore departed for a season, that thou shouldest receive him for ever;

16 Not now as a servant, but above a servant, a brother beloved, specially to me, but how much more unto thee, both in the flesh, and in the Lord?

17 If thou count me therefore a partner, receive him as myself.

18 If he hath wronged thee, or oweth *thee* aught, put that on mine account;

19 I Paul have written *it* with mine own hand, I will repay *it:* albeit I do not say to thee how thou owest unto me even thine own self besides.

20 Yea, brother, let me have joy of thee in the Lord: refresh my bowels in the Lord.

21 Having confidence in thy obedience I wrote unto thee, knowing that thou wilt also do more than I say.

22 But withal prepare me also a lodging: for I trust that through your prayers I shall be given unto you.

23 There salute thee Epaphras, my fellow prisoner in Christ Jesus;

24 Marcus, Aristarchus, Demas, Lucas, my fellow labourers.

25 The grace of our Lord Jesus Christ *be* with your spirit. Amen.

To reconcile—the mark of a leader led by God.

No man can produce great things who is not thoroughly sincere in dealing with himself.

—James Russell Lowell

There is no better test for a man's ultimate integrity than his behavior when he is wrong.

—Unknown

No man was ever great without divine inspiration.

—Cicero

As I grow older, I pay less attention to what men say. I just watch what they do.

—Andrew Carnegie

If thou wouldst conquer thy weakness thou must not gratify it.

—William Penn

The day is always his who worked in it with serenity and great aims.

—Ralph Waldo Emerson

The identifying of values to which we can all give allegiance is a light preliminary exercise before the real and heroic task: to make the values live. Values have been carved on monuments and spelled out in illuminated manuscripts. We do not need more of that. They must be made to live in the acts of men.

—John Gardner

It takes a wise man to recognize a wise man.

—Xenophenes

James

1 My brethren, be not many masters, knowing that we shall receive the greater condemnation.

2 For in many things we offend all. If any man offend not in word, the same *is* a perfect man, *and* able also to bridle the whole body.

3 Behold, we put bits in the horses' mouths, that they may obey us; and we turn about their whole body.

4 Behold also the ships, which though *they be* so great, and *are* driven of fierce winds, yet are they turned about with a very small helm, whithersoever the governor listeth.

5 Even so the tongue is a little member, and boasteth great things. Behold, how great a matter a little fire kindleth!

6 And the tongue *is* a fire, a world of iniquity: so is the tongue among our members, that it defileth the whole body, and setteth on fire the course of nature; and it is set on fire of hell.

7 For every kind of beasts, and of birds, and of serpents, and of things in the sea, is tamed, and hath been tamed of mankind:

8 But the tongue can no man tame; *it is* an unruly evil, full of deadly poison.

9 Therewith bless we God, even the Father; and therewith curse we men, which are made after the similitude of God.

10 Out of the same mouth proceedeth blessing and cursing. My brethren, these things ought not so to be.

11 Doth a fountain send forth at the same place sweet *water* and bitter?

12 Can the fig tree, my brethren, bear olive berries? either a vine, figs? so *can* no fountain both yield salt water and fresh.

13 Who *is* a wise man and endued with knowledge among you? let him shew out of a good conversation his works with meekness of wisdom.

14 But if ye have bitter envying and strife in your hearts, glory not, and lie not against the truth.

15 This wisdom descendeth not from above, but *is* earthly, sensual, devilish.

16 For where envying and strife *is,* there *is* confusion and every evil work.

17 But the wisdom that is from above is first pure, then peaceable, gentle, *and* easy to be intreated, full of mercy and good fruits, without partiality, and without hypocrisy.

18 And the fruit of righteousness is sown in peace of them that make peace.

Ask God to teach you what to say and how to listen.

Reflections